Mark

INTERPRETATION
BIBLE STUDIES

Mark

RICHARD I. DEIBERT

Geneva Press
Louisville, Kentucky

This book belongs to the long-suffering fall 1998 Kerygma Bible Study Class of Immanuel Presbyterian Church in Montgomery, Alabama, for whom the Word of God remains a lamp unto their feet and a light unto their path: Macky and Wiley Boyles, Nancy and Rock Chambless, Betty Conner, Deborah Day, Coke Ellington, Barbara Grant, Hannah Harrell, Nan Hughes, Eddie Johnson, Carolyn King, Sue and George Lauderbaugh, Ruth Liddell, Helen Moore, Mary Moore, Beth Nicholson, Anne and Dave Patten, Calli Patterson, Shirley Scarbrough, Ruth Steffen, and Frances Sutton.

© 1999 Richard I. Deibert
Leader's Guide © 1998 Geneva Press

Book design by Sharon Adams
Cover design by Pam Poll
Cover illustration by Robert Stratton

First edition
Published by Geneva Press
Louisville, Kentucky

This book is printed on acid-free paper that meets the American National Standards Institute Z39.48 standard. ♾

PRINTED IN THE UNITED STATES OF AMERICA

99 00 01 02 03 04 05 06 07 08 — 10 9 8 7 6 5 4 3 2 1

Library of Congress Cataloging-in-Publication Data

A catalog record for this book is available from the Library of Congress.

ISBN 0-664-50078-1

Contents

Series Introduction

The Bible has long been revered for its witness to God's presence and redeeming activity in the world; its message of creation and judgment, love and forgiveness, grace and hope; its memorable characters and stories; its challenges to human life; and its power to shape faith. For generations people have found in the Bible inspiration and instruction, and, for nearly as long, commentators and scholars have assisted students of the Bible. This series, Interpretation Bible Studies (IBS), continues that great heritage of scholarship with a fresh approach to biblical study.

Designed for ease and flexibility of use for either personal or group study, IBS helps readers not only to learn about the history and theology of the Bible, understand the sometimes difficult language of biblical passages, and marvel at the biblical accounts of God's activity in human life, but also to accept the challenge of the Bible's call to discipleship. IBS offers sound guidance for deepening one's knowledge of the Bible and for faithful Christian living in today's world.

IBS was developed out of three primary convictions. First, the Bible is the church's scripture and stands in a unique place of authority in Christian understanding. Second, good scholarship helps readers understand the truths of the Bible and sharpens their perception of God speaking through the Bible. Third, deep knowledge of the Bible bears fruit in one's ethical and spiritual life.

Each IBS volume has ten brief units of key passages from a book of the Bible. By moving through these units, readers capture the sweep of the whole biblical book. Each unit includes study helps, such as maps, photos, definitions of key terms, questions for reflection, and suggestions for resources for further study. In the back of each volume is a Leader's Guide that offers helpful suggestions on how to use IBS.

The Interpretation Bible Studies series grows out of the well-known Interpretation commentaries (John Knox Press), a series that helps preachers and teachers in their preparation. Although each IBS volume bears a deep kinship to its companion Interpretation commentary, IBS can stand alone. The reader need not be familiar with the Interpretation commentary to benefit from IBS. However, those who want to discover even more about the Bible will benefit by consulting Interpretation commentaries too.

Through the kind of encounter with the Bible encouraged by the Interpretation Bible Studies, the church will continue to discover God speaking afresh in the scriptures.

Introduction to Mark

Welcome. You have chosen to study the Gospel according to Mark. Perhaps your pastor is preaching on a passage from Mark and you wish to come prepared to worship. Perhaps you are new to Christian faith and wish to hear the story of Jesus Christ in its earliest telling. Perhaps you are a seasoned student of scripture and this is one more book for you to devour. Whatever your reason for tackling Mark, you have made a courageous decision. Mark will not be easy.

Mark will not be easy for two reasons. First, Mark is a sophisticated artist. He paints his Gospel of Jesus Christ with strokes that are demanding on the viewer. He veils the rich truth of Jesus Christ behind irony, allusion, terseness, juxtaposition, repetition, silence, and abruption. So come to this Gospel with an eager mind, for Mark will stretch—and satisfy—every interpretive muscle. As with good art, if the viewer is available for transformation, he or she must stand before it with patience. In time, the Word will become flesh.

> **1** The beginning of the good news[a] of Jesus Christ, the Son of God.[b]
> 2 As it is written in the prophet Isaiah,[c]
>> "See, I am sending my messenger
>> ahead of you,[d]
>> who will prepare your way;
> 3 the voice of one crying out in the wilderness:
>> 'Prepare the way of the Lord,
>> make his paths straight,' "

The second reason Mark will not be easy is because Christian discipleship is not easy. Whether "Mark" is a pastor of one congregation, a pastor for several congregations, or—as is more likely—a collective pastor, he has experienced the trials and tribulations of fainthearted disciples in the rough and tumble of the first century. Mark tends to portray Christian discipleship as an all-or-nothing phenomenon, with consequences that are not immediately pretty. At the same time, he consistently maintains that no other human decision is more necessary and worthwhile.

What Is a Gospel?

Mark is the shortest Gospel, Mark is the only Gospel to actually call itself "Gospel," and Mark is generally agreed to be the first Gospel. For us moderns, living more than five hundred years after the Gutenberg Bible, this is not so impressive. But for Mark, deciding to write a Gospel was a daring decision. The world knew no such literature as Gospel prior to Mark's decision. The world knew story, but a Gospel is more than story. The world knew biography, but a Gospel is more than biography. The world knew history, but a Gospel is more than history. The world knew hero-tale, but a Gospel is more than hero-tale. Prior to Mark, the form of literature we know as Gospel did not exist. In our best estimation, Mark pioneered the Gospel form.

So what is a Gospel? Most know that the word "Gospel" means something like "good news." Unfortunately, for most of us the term "good news" has become tired. Perhaps we attend so much to bad news these days that the meaning of "good news" has diminished beyond recognition. The word "Gospel" is more accurately translated "glad tidings" and carries the emotional content of a cry of joy. Think of it this way, you have chosen to study *the Cry of Joy about Jesus Christ, the Son of God,* according to Mark.

Who was Mark?

Though an older tradition associates this Gospel with John Mark, a companion of Paul, most modern scholarship concedes that the author is unknown. For more information, see Joel B. Green, Scot McKnight, and I. Howard Marshall, eds., *Dictionary of Jesus and the Gospels* (Downers Grove, Ill.: InterVarsity Press, 1992), 514.

As an art form, a Gospel falls somewhere in the neighborhood of sermon and sacrament. A sermon uses words to teach, proclaim, and define, but contains a larger purpose. A sacrament uses symbols to recollect, represent, and communicate, but contains a larger purpose. Mark's new literary effort is both sermon-like and sacrament-like. Mark hopes to draw his listeners personally into the narrative so that they themselves stand face-to-face with Jesus Christ, experiencing

him as the Twelve experienced him. Mark wants his listeners to res-
onate with the same dilemmas, choices, failures, confusion, anxiety,
and joy as the original Twelve. Suffice it to say, Mark writes not to get
us to hear his cry of joy about Jesus Christ; he writes to get us to *utter* the cry of joy ourselves.

A Map for the Journey

The design of this series, Interpretation Bible Studies, is particularly
challenging to books of the Bible that are narratives. Narratives seek
to provide a perceptible continuity to the reader. Reducing a complex
narrative like the Gospel of Mark to a study of ten passages can compromise Mark's narrative continuity and its comprehensive force.
Therefore, let us be diligent readers.

Let us read the entire narrative aloud before beginning any of these
units—preferably aloud in a group—to avail ourselves of the richness
of different inflections. Then, before plunging headlong into any specific unit, let us read around the passage that is covered, studying the
larger context of the story before studying the substance of the individual passage. Mark made a host of artistic decisions regarding beginning, ending, order, and sequence. The overall arrangement of
Mark's Gospel is simple, as shown in the outline below. However,
each major section of narrative carries distinct emphases, tones, and
technique. As we study, note where we are along the Marcan journey.
Let us keep the biblical text in view while making this study. The New
Revised Standard Version (NRSV) and the author's personal translations are used frequently, but any nonparaphrased translation will do.
This study follows the Greek text and so it will be helpful to main-
tain close contact with a good English translation. And let us be hon-
est readers. Ask the questions of your heart and your mind. Argue
with the author. Argue with the church. Argue with the text. Argue
with God.

The following outline is a simplified outline of Mark's whole
Gospel. Think of it as a map of the entire country in which we will be
traveling. Along the way, we will make just ten stops in this country
of Mark. At each stop, we will try to experience the whole country by
drinking deeply of that particular site. As we bury ourselves in the local culture of each passage, it will help now and then to glance back at
this map to remind ourselves where we are in the country as a whole.

	Outline	
I.	Mark 1:1–15	Beginning
II.	Mark 1:16–8:26	Galilee
III.	Mark 8:22–10:52	Between Galilee and Jerusalem
IV.	Mark 11:1–15:47	Jerusalem
V.	Mark 16:1–8	Ending

Signposts along the Way

For further reading on the Gospel of Mark, see Lamar Williamson, Jr., *Mark*, Interpretation (Atlanta: John Knox Press, 1983); Douglas R. A. Hare, *Mark*, Westminster Bible Companion (Louisville, Ky.: Westminster John Knox Press, 1996); and William Barclay, *The Gospel of Mark*, Daily Study Bible (Philadelphia: Westminster Press, 1975).

Once more, please read aloud the entire Gospel before commencing this study. Not only will this sensitize you to the context of each passage, but reading the entire Gospel in one sitting will help you avoid "cross-pollinating" Mark's telling with Matthew's telling, or Luke's, or even John's. Cross-pollination occurs when a detail unique to another's story is subconsciously (or consciously) carried over and deposited in Mark's story, even though Mark did not tell the story that way. Cross-pollinating *can* help sometimes, but it also can diminish the artistry and distinctiveness of Mark's story.

As you read the entire narrative aloud, note Mark's unique manner of telling. Watch for the following twists, turns, and techniques that Mark uses:

- Suddenness and immediacy—the word group for "immediately" occurs more than forty times and accelerates the pace of the narrative; there is even a sudden beginning and a sudden ending
- The use of mighty acts to highlight a powerful, deed-oriented Jesus, rather than a creed-oriented Jesus
- Jesus' slightly diminished role as a teacher, with fewer words of teaching than in the other Gospel accounts
- A vivid, concrete, and detailed—but apparently clumsy—narrative prose
- A juxtapositional narrative that sometimes appears uncon-

cerned with flow or transition, where events and moments often stand—side-by-side—in stark contrast

- The way the end of the story functions as the center of gravity, drawing the story relentlessly toward itself
- The occurrence of doublets (two of a kinds, e.g., water and bread miracles), threefold patterns (e.g., seed parables, passion predictions, denials), and stories sandwiched within other stories
- The peculiar way Mark reveals Jesus by hiding him ("messianic secrecy"), usually marked by phrases like "See that you say nothing to no one," and "He strictly ordered them that no one should know this"
- The inverse character development—as the narrative progresses, Jesus' character becomes fuller while those of his disciples diminish
- The dramatically different character of Jesus' public ministry in Galilee and his private ministry in Jerusalem
- The occurrence of different titles for Jesus and who uses them—for example, "Messiah," "Son of David," and "Son of God" in the mouths of others, and "Son of Man" almost exclusively in Jesus' mouth

Have Fun

Above all, have fun with the Bible! The author of this study comes from a faith tradition which states without embarrassment that our "chief and highest end" as human beings is "to glorify God, and fully to enjoy God forever" (Westminster Larger Catechism, Q. 1). There is no better way to fully enjoy God than to delight in the sacred text with friends along the way. In fact, it can be rapturous! As the Jewish Talmud gleefully urges, "Turn it, turn it, turn it." To sit with dour disposition before such art as the Bible is an ingratitude of the worst kind.

When church officers are selected, they are sometimes asked: "Will you

Want to Know More?

About the development of the Gospels? See William M. Ramsay, *The Westminster Guide to the Books of the Bible* (Louisville, Ky.: Westminster John Knox Press, 1994), 289–316; John Barton, *How the Bible Came to Be* (Louisville, Ky.: Westminster John Knox Press, 1998), 18–22, 44–46; Archibald M. Hunter, *Introducing the New Testament*, 3d rev. ed. (Philadelphia: Westminster Press, 1973), 23–26.

About the content or themes of each Gospel? See Duncan S. Ferguson, *Bible Basics: Mastering the Content of the Bible* (Louisville, Ky.: Westminster John Knox Press, 1995), 57–65; Hunter, *Introducing the New Testament*, 37–70.

seek to serve the people with energy, intelligence, imagination, and love?" Nowhere is this a more pertinent question than with our attitude toward the Bible. If you feel like arguing with what you read, then gird up your loins and *argue*! If you feel intellectually provoked, *think*! If you feel inspired, *dream*! If you feel the heart of God beat for you, then find someone and *love*!

But for heaven's sake, do not allow yourself, or the church, the disservice of passionless study.

> Euagelio (that we cal gospel) is a greke worde,
> and signyfyth good, mery, glad and joyfull tydings,
> that maketh a mannes hert glad,
> and maketh him synge, daunce and leepe for ioye.[1]

---

[1] The words of William Tyndale, the English Reformer (c. 1492-1536), who was burned at the stake for his subversive effort to translate the Bible into English, in his *Prologue to the New Testament*, 1525. Quoted in Hugh T. Kerr, *The Simple Gospel: Reflections on Christian Faith* (Louisville, Ky.: Westminster/John Knox Press, 1991), 72.

The Mystery Appears

Mark begins his story about Jesus Christ with striking force. Before we are fifteen verses into the narrative, we are aware this moment in history is a central moment for the world. All that has gone before has tilted mysteriously toward this moment; from this time forward, all that will happen will look back.

Mark believes that "time-within-time" has been realized in the event of Jesus Christ. So he crafts his beginning to convey an ironic mixture of patience and urgency. His style instills within us a distinct sense that while God has been patiently waiting for this particular time in the world, once history swelled to this moment, God acted immediately and urgently. Thus Mark writes with a style and pace that convey seriousness. For him, Jesus Christ is God's supreme movement toward the world. This peculiar human being from Nazareth ultimately addresses our deepest fears about life and death.

Mark wastes no narrative. He accomplishes in fifteen verses what Matthew and Luke more leisurely accomplish across several chapters. When we arrive at the first concrete event in Jesus' public ministry, in verses 14–15, we already know that this particular Jew and his mission stand on the prophetic authority of Israel, the verbal authentication of heaven, the ministry of angels, and the conviction of personal testimony. Jamming four persuasive scenes side-by-side, Mark deftly creates within us a keen anticipation that this will be the greatest story ever told.

Mark is also a pastor who understands that when we engage his story of Jesus Christ, we will *be* engaged by the bittersweet story of our own incapacity to trust the goodness of God. Mark has already been where this narrative will take us. He knows the cost of following Jesus Christ day-by-day and the pain of failing to pay that price. He knows that the contentment of leisurely discipleship is but a mirage, and that the satisfaction of grace-taken-for-granted is fleeting. In this way, we can see that the author, "Mark," is likely a *community* of Christians that has experienced time and again the painful miracle of God's faithfulness. They have come to understand through the fire of experience that the Lord they continue to fail nevertheless fails them not.

"Prepare the way. . . . Make God's paths straight."

So at the outset of his narrative journey, Mark hands us this résumé of testimonies to Jesus Christ. Mark knows we will become frightened as we engage the demonic powers within his narrative in the context of our lives. He knows we will begin to doubt as we encounter the cunning religious professionals. And he knows, above all, that we will ultimately fail to travel where Jesus calls us.

Mark knows this, yet hopes against hope that if this prologue can attach itself to our imagination, we might tread this dangerous way in the presence of one who has been here before.

The Title (1:1)

So wedded are we to the birth stories of Jesus that we likely miss the impact of Mark's opening verse. We are so taken by magi and shepherds, pregnant virgins, and inns with no vacancies that we tend to overlook the marquee placed so carefully above the stage of this extraordinary narrative. Mark cannot raise the curtain without first signaling the cosmic sweep of the drama to come.

No other Gospel writer begins like this. Perhaps this is because Mark did it first. The "title" in verse 1 could be translated, "An Authentic Telling of the Glad Tidings about Jesus Christ, the Son of God," as if to say, "This News about Jesus Christ, God's Own, is Gladdening News, with Original Authority."

Here at the start it is vital to understand that the word "gospel" is not strictly a New Testament word, as if only the newer Testament lays claim to the good tidings of God. In verse 2 Mark names the prophet Isaiah, whose book the early church was reading in the Greek Bible of the Jews, known as the Septuagint, rather than in the Hebrew. Mark is aware that when his readers hear the Greek word "gospel" (*euangelion*) in the very first sentence, their hearts will ring with Isaiah's announcement of survival, freedom, and homecoming for exiled Israel:

> Go up a high mountain, you who proclaim *gospel* to Zion. Lift high your voice with strength, you who proclaim *gospel* to Jerusalem. Lift it up, do not fear. Say to the cities of Judah: "Behold, your God!" (Isa. 40:9, Septuagint)

Mark's choice of the word "gospel" in his opening sentence—his marquee—is meant to sound within the church's soul the glorious news that God's Son, Jesus Christ, is our guarantee of survival, freedom, and homecoming:

> Go up a high mountain, church. Lift high your voice with strength, church. Lift it up, do not fear. Say to the world: "Behold, Jesus Christ!" (Isa. 40:9)

The Preaching of John (1:2–8)

Mark's narrative properly begins with verse 2. Like all writers, Mark had to think deeply about the beginning of his story. Surely he asked himself, "What must I emphasize? What can my reader not afford to miss?" These were the same strategic literary concerns facing Mark.

How important it is, then, to recognize that Mark begins his story by anchoring the glad tidings of Jesus Christ in the prophetic tradition of Isaiah. Matthew begins by locating Jesus within a particular genealogy, Luke begins by locating Jesus within a particular historical reign, while Mark begins by locating Jesus within a particular Hebrew prophet, Isaiah. This Gospel, with relatively the fewest references to the Hebrew Scripture, launches itself with a quote from the most beloved of Israel's prophets.

Now imagine, it has been several centuries since the close of the historic prophetic period for Israel. For Jews, life turns into wilderness whenever mediators, messengers, and mouthpieces of the Lord go missing. To lose all tether to the Holy One and to be left to its own wisdom is for Israel to exist in an intolerable state of wildness. We may assume here in this wilderness between the testaments that Israel was craning its neck to the breaking point for even the slightest voice from on high.

> "The text can still encounter every hearer in the emptiness of his or her wilderness. . . . The voice of a rough and roaring prophet can still call the hearer to turn around, accept the greater baptism offered by a risen Lord, and thus experience his coming as a powerful, personal advent."—Williamson, *Mark*, Interpretation, 33.

What Mark wants his hearers to experience at the very beginning of this story is the sheer elation of Jews at a voice crying out in the wilderness, a voice acknowledging their existence, certifying their worth, and promising their deliverance. Mark wishes to evoke within us the exhilaration of being noticed after hope has been cast aside. So he joins a messianic text from Malachi to a homecoming text from Isaiah and declares, "You have been seen! You have been seen in the wilderness! At long last, the drifting is over! Rise and prepare the way of the Lord!" (1:2–3).

Using these prophetic texts, Mark directs us to John, the crusty, Isaiah-like figure, who is waiting in the wilderness, as we are. John seems obsessed with baptism, a Jewish rite of cleansing for Gentile converts. Not only do we find John immersing the entire populations of Judea and Jerusalem (!), but we hear him preaching to them about the urgency of being immersed. However he understands it, John perceives baptism to be the principal reason for the advent of Jesus Christ in the world. John will tell us that, compared to Jesus, he is profoundly subservient in person and in practice. John is a model of humility.

At this point, the church often commits a grave and costly error. Sometimes we do not see that John-the-Baptizer is *not* at cross-purposes with Jesus-the-Baptizer. The text as Mark presents it would make no sense if the ministry of John and Jesus were contradicting. In some circles, however, John's ministry is depicted as opposing Jesus' ministry, as if John and Jesus have completely different

"I have baptized you with water; but he will baptize you with the Holy Spirit."

theologies! Invariably, this course of thought leads to anti-Semitism. Mark would be horrified to hear any characterization of John as an Old Covenant witness to a God who loves with condition, and Jesus as a New Covenant witness to a God who loves without condition.

The church cannot afford to mistake John's exemplary humility before Jesus for a divergence in theology from Jesus. John and Jesus are both devout Jews. They share the same scripture. They worship the God of Abraham and Sarah. And they are both preaching a baptism of repentance *into* the forgiveness of sins. Thus Mark lands us in one of the densest minefields in theology.

Lamar Williamson, Jr., (31–32) rightly warns that the translation of this phrase bristles with difficulty. Williamson states the issue concisely: Does John mean that baptism is a *means to* God's forgiveness or that baptism is a *sign of* God's forgiveness? If the former, baptism actually makes forgiveness real; it is the *condition* required for forgiveness. If the latter, baptism expresses what is already real; it is the *proof* of forgiveness. The Greek preposition (*eis*), translated "for" in the New Revised Standard Version ("a baptism of repentance *for* the forgiveness of sins"), can also be accurately translated "into" ("a baptism of repentance *into* the forgiveness of sins"), resulting in theologies that are massively different.

> "The amazing thing about John's baptism was that he, a Jew, was asking Jews to submit to that which only a Gentile was supposed to need."—Barclay, *The Gospel of Mark*, Daily Study Bible, 14.

Read in the context of Mark's prologue, John can only be calling sinners to turn from their disobedience and to immerse (or baptize) themselves in God's *pre-existing* reality of forgiveness. The tone of John's preaching (often mischaracterized as angry) more likely resounded with joy: "Hear the glad tidings of God: your sins have been forgiven! The one coming behind me will make this abundantly clear. Your sins have been forgiven! Turn and live like forgiven people! Drown your sins in God's mercy! Reform yourselves!"

Williamson (32) draws on John Calvin to emphasize the importance of this distinction. Of the Reformers, Calvin wrestled as vigorously as any with the relationship between repentance, baptism, and forgiveness. This is not to say that Calvin ultimately got it right, but that Calvin knew what could *not* be said:

> Repentance is not placed first, as some ignorantly suppose, as if it were the ground of the forgiveness of sins, or as if it induced God to begin

to be gracious to us; but [we] are commanded to repent, that [we] may receive the reconciliation which is offered to [us]. (Calvin, 179).

So for Mark, John the Baptizer is a vital link between Israel and the church, between Jews and Christians, and between Judaism and Christianity. And for us, John the Baptizer is also a vital link between the Old and New Testaments. He must, indeed, be distinguished from Jesus in his person and whisked from the stage when the time is right, but we can in no way construe John as being opposed to the essential mission of Jesus.

Make no mistake, this story is the *good* news about Jesus Christ, who is the Son of the God of Abraham and Sarah. John is the voice in our wilderness, crying out with jubilation that the Lord of Israel's forgiveness has come, and that it is crucial to live as if this is so.

The Baptism of Jesus (1:9-11)

With no further ado, enter Jesus. Why waste time? We know Jesus is the main character. John the Baptizer has laid the red carpet of Israel's faith. Let's get on with it.

All Mark tells us is that this Jesus comes from Nazareth, a town in the region of Galilee. Mark's introduction is more like eavesdropping. Jesus submits to John as if by instinct. The Son of God is baptized in the Jordan.

Here we pause and reflect on the naturalness of Jesus' baptism and the theological consistency of it in Mark's hands. If baptism *into* forgiveness (John's proclamation) means that baptism is the *condition* for God's forgiveness, then why on earth would Jesus Christ, Son of God, seek to satisfy such a condition? On the other hand, if baptism *into* forgiveness means that baptism *signifies* forgiveness—attests to, expresses, aligns with, and seals what already is—then is baptism not completely natural for the Son of God who comes to "give his life a ransom for many" (Mark 10:45, NRSV), as an act of personal identification with God's glorious will to redeem?

The ensuing picture of Jesus' baptism is graphic. The Son comes up; the Spirit comes down; the Father speaks tenderly. Jesus sees and hears and feels it all. While we should not make too much out of the observation that this particular baptism involves Father, Son, and Spirit, we should not ignore it either. Besides the element of water, the only universal in baptism throughout Christian history is its occurrence "in the name of the Father, and of the Son, and of the Holy Spirit." Could Mark be suggesting that in this particular baptism rests the essential meaning of all baptism?

Again, we are inclined to think of Jesus' baptism as theologically distinct from ours. It most certainly is not! Mark writes this Gospel for folk like us who struggle with discipleship. Mark knows that what we need more than anything for our discipleship is the certainty of covenantal belonging, not the nagging threat of conditionalism. Mark's purpose in the baptism of Jesus Christ is to convey his identity. Jesus needs to know who he is, but so do Jesus' disciples. As the Messiah is immersed into God's covenant of mercy, the church that follows him is likewise immersed. As Jesus learns of his Sonship and belovedness and pleasure within the heart of God, so do we learn of ours. In the thundering whisper of Jesus' identity, we hear the truth about ourselves, "Beloved sons and daughters, with whom God is absolutely delighted" (v. 11).

> "This is a secret epiphany. Jesus knows who he is by means of an experience that is not accessible to objective, public verification. Others must discover this truth by listening to what Jesus says and by watching what he does."—Williamson, *Mark*, Interpretation, 35.

This is precisely what the church gives us in baptism: the truth about ourselves, the bedrock of our identity, the sole foundation for discipleship, our only reliable hope in the midst of despair. "You—*you* personally—are God's child, beloved and pleasing to God. This is your definition; your truth amidst all lies; living proof that you ultimately matter" (v. 11).

The Test of Jesus (1:12–13)

In a jarring transition, Mark next juxtaposes Jesus' baptism with his wilderness experience. Jesus has received his glorious baptismal identity and, a split second later, is hurled into the wilderness to be examined. The Spirit, having just come down on him, throws him into the ring with Satan.

The witness here is embarrassingly bald. There is no question who is responsible. There is no question why. There is also no fasting or hunger or three-point debate. And there is no sense of victory. This famous scene is minimal in Mark's drama. It is simply Jesus vs. Satan before a gallery of wild beasts and angels. Mark refuses to even tell us explicitly whether Jesus passes the test! There is only the subtle suggestion that were his resources not from heaven, he could not have survived on his own. Utter dependency on God is the modus operandi of the baptized.

Here in the Beloved Son we learn of our own baptismal struggle. Williamson (39) recognizes that phenomenologically "the onslaught of Satan is strongest just after the exhilaration of a moment of revelation." Mark leaves us with little doubt that the moment we are named in baptism—pronounced as beloved and belonging—we too will find ourselves in a wilderness struggle for identity. Mark has been there. He knows how inhospitable this existence can be for the baptized. Mark has felt in his body both the tearing of earth's wild beasts and the ministry of heaven's angels. Mark knows that the way of disciples is no different than the way of the teacher.

Want to Know More?

About John the Baptist? See Paul J. Achtemeier, ed., *Harper's Bible Dictionary* (San Francisco: Harper & Row, 1985), 501–2.

About the Septuagint? See Celia Brewer Marshall, *A Guide Through the Old Testament* (Louisville, Ky.: Westminster John Knox Press, 1989), 20; J. Alberto Soggin, *Introduction to the Old Testament*, 3d ed., Old Testament Library (Louisville, Ky.: Westminster John Knox Press, 1989), 23–26.

About messianic expectations? See Celia Brewer Marshall, *A Guide Through the New Testament* (Louisville, Ky.: Westminster John Knox Press, 1994), 33.

About the baptism of Jesus? For a thorough, though technical, discussion on the historic understandings of the reasons for Jesus' baptism, see George R. Beasley-Murray, *Baptism in the New Testament* (Grand Rapids: Wm. B. Eerdmans Publishing Co., 1973), 45–67.

About different understandings of baptism? See Alan Richardson and John Bowden, eds., *The Westminster Dictionary of Christian Theology* (Philadelphia: Westminster Press, 1983), 299–302; J. G. Davies, ed., *The Westminster Dictionary of Liturgy and Worship* (Philadelphia: Westminster Press, 1986), 55–77; Ted A. Campbell, *Christian Confession: A Historical Introduction* (Louisville, Ky.: Westminster John Knox Press, 1996).

The Gospel of God (1:14–15)

Evidently, Jesus passes the test, for in the next verses we find him preaching his first sermon. And it's a humdinger (and a lesson for all preachers): one sentence with three clauses.

Now Mark removes John the Baptizer from the stage. John's influence will continue to be felt, but Mark makes it clear that John's place front-and-center has changed forever. Mark writes as if we should be expecting this, indeed, as if John's arrest has been known before the ages.

Do not overlook this Markan touch! With a single passing phrase, Mark signals a changing of the epochs. All has been readied. The paths have been made straight. "Elijah" has served his calling. Now he is whisked away stage-left and Jesus enters stage-right. He is baptized, tested, robed, and preaching. Mark has brought us to the center of the history of the world.

Once again, we learn at this critical moment that the news Jesus bears from God is thoroughly *good*. If we are not careful, we will glide right through the narrator's voice on our way to the kingdom without hearing this important reminder that what Jesus bears in his person is gospel—glad tidings. It's the same word at the center of verse 1, the marquee for the entire drama. There, in front of the drama, the church of old has signaled that this is a drama of the glad tidings of *Jesus*. Here, inside the drama, Jesus is telling us it's a drama of the glad tidings of *God*. In sum, the church proclaims a proclaimer; our good news about Jesus is his good news about God.

What Jesus says is not exactly a model of clarity for preaching. He is obviously wrestling with material that eludes concreteness. To describe this moment in history, Jesus does not choose the common Greek word for linear, chronological time as the clock sees it (*chronos*). Jesus chooses the special Greek word for seasonal, appointed-though-unpredictable time, as the Clockmaker sees it, perhaps best translated "time-within-time" (*kairos*). To make matters muddier, Jesus chooses to speak with a wonderfully rich tense in Greek, the perfect tense, which is used to indicate that the effects of a past action are still continuing in the present. So a paraphrase of the first half of Jesus' sermon might run like this:

> Time-within-time has begun to ripen and ripens now,
> God has begun to reign in this world and reigns now. . . .

Said like this, Jesus packs a punch! In fact, if Williamson (40) is right and these first words of Jesus set forth "in a broader sense . . . the theme of the entire story," a gasp of astonishment becomes the only sensible response. After all, is not a glimpse of heaven the universal fantasy? Who would not pay a great price to peek into heavenly existence for reassurance that there will be food for all, that disease and pestilence will not stalk us, that arrogance, pride, and greed will not infest our relationships? Who is there, with any sensibility whatsoever, who does not crave even the merest acquaintance with the person and personableness of the living God?

> **Time's Up**
>
> "Whenever the gospel is faithfully preached . . . the kingdom of God draws near to the hearers."—Williamson, *Mark*, Interpretation, 42.

Amazingly, Jesus proclaims that the moment all humanity has been waiting for has arrived. The universal fantasy need no longer be a fantasy. Heaven is kissing earth! The rule of God can actually be seen, heard, touched, and known, here and now.

While Jesus in Mark's account would never claim direct responsibility for the ripening of time and the arrival of God's rule, surely he had grown aware of its mysterious overlap with his person. Jesus confidently proclaims that the moment defining all moments (*kairos*) has been ushered to the world's stage. Being neither boastful nor arrogant, Jesus is certain it is now.

As the church meanders through Mark's narrative from this point on, Mark wants us to recognize the rule of almighty God in the life, love, and longing of this Jesus from Nazareth. Mark wants us to receive the sum of Jesus' ministry—his mighty deeds, his dignifying care, his wise instruction, his laughter and anger, his tears of joy and lament—as an accurate picture of God personally reigning among us. Mark would have us bring our curiosity and longing—and all our questions about God—to this story about Jesus Christ; and he would have us press them into the story until they are answered.

For Mark, the glorious news is that in Jesus' mysterious person God's long-awaited reign on earth had begun, and was continuing in Mark's day, and is continuing in ours. To see Jesus battle demons from a grave-dweller's body is to know that demons even within a grave-dweller contradict the desire of God. To see Jesus conquer the forces of nature to quell fishermen's fear is to know that fear for one's survival contradicts the will of God. To see Jesus remobilize a paralyzed body or restore a withered limb is to know that the Creator God most surely wills the creation to work by its design. To see Jesus alarmed over divorce or pride or lust is to know of God's alarm over the way these can tear the delicate fabric of life. To see Jesus awaken a girl from the sleep of death is to know that God wills the fullness of human life and potential.

Mark has experienced God's reign in Jesus' person and writes to transfer this experience to us. In Williamson's words (41), "Those who are confronted by the power of God in the words and works of Jesus experience the kingdom as present, yet hidden; its full manifestation still lies in a future that has drawn near." While it is true that we see through a mirror dimly, Mark had learned nevertheless that we actually see.

It is the awesome goodness of God that beats at the heart of Jesus' mission. Throughout this prologue, emphasis has been placed on the continuity and constancy of God's purpose in the life of Israel and John the Baptizer. The mission that Israel and John have shared is to call humanity into the transforming reality of God's mercy. It is identical to the mission of Jesus Christ. The difference between Israel and

John and Jesus is not in their mission, but in their *person*. Israel and John and Jesus all testify to the good news of God, like voices in a symphony. But it is in Jesus Christ's *person* alone that the good news of God actually *exists*.

On this foundation, Jesus commands the church to repent, to re-form its lifestyle. Then he issues a second, often overlooked command: "Trust God's goodness." The God of mercy reigns here on earth in our life together, now. The time for decision will therefore, from this moment on, always be now. It makes no sense with God now among us to do anything except align our whole selves with God's rule. Like the needle of a compass pulled by a great magnetic field, our moral lives should be swinging round toward the God of mercy. We should realign our prideful posturings, recalibrate our ethical thresholds, and remanufacture our principled priorities.

> "Whenever we affirm our baptism, we acknowledge God's right to rule, and we accept the commission to anticipate the kingdom of God by the way we live day by day."—Hare, *Mark*, Westminster Bible Companion, 19.

Jesus knows, however, that unless we see a good and merciful God behind, beneath, and above all this, we will be weakly motivated to change. So, in what Williamson (42) sees as "the climax of the appeal," Jesus commands us to trust the gospel, to let go, and to lean into the glad tidings of God, trusting that we will be caught. "To be seen, [the good news of God] must be believed" (Williamson, 42). If we will fully know, we must fully release ourselves.

Repent and believe. Reform and trust. Do it now, not later. But do it because the news God has for you is good.

? Questions for Reflection

1. The Gospel of Mark begins with the words, "The beginning of the good news." What does it mean by "good news"? Why is that good news? Is it still good news today? Why or why not?
2. Mark begins with a quote from Isaiah about a voice in the wilderness, moves to John who is baptizing in the wilderness, and then on to Jesus who is baptized, as if a baton is being passed from the prophets down to Jesus. Who are the individuals who have passed their baton to you? In whose line of tradition do you stand?
3. There is a sense of geographical movement in the biblical text.

John comes from the wilderness to the Jordan river, Jesus comes from Galilee to the Jordan, and then Jesus is thrust out into the wilderness (only next to return to Galilee). Mark may be suggesting a theological significance to these locations. In fact, the last reference made about Jesus in the Gospel is that he is "going ahead of you to Galilee" (Mark 16:7, NRSV). Using a good Bible dictionary, look up words like "wilderness" or "desert," "river" or "Jordan River," and "Galilee." What do your findings suggest to you about the journeys of Jesus to these locations? Where are the wildernesses, the Jordans, and the Galilees in your life?

4. Mark 1:15 (NRSV) states that, "The time is fulfilled," as if to say, "*The* time is here." What is the most important time you can think of? (A wedding, a birth, a first job, etc.) What preparation would you make for that moment? What difference would it make if you found out that special time has already begun?

The Mystery Discriminates

A great deal has happened since Jesus' first sermon in chapter 1 (1:14–15). He has launched his ministry with what could be called reckless abandon. Nowhere else in any of the Gospels do we find Jesus engaged in such a flurry of activity as we do in Mark's hands between chapters 1 and 3.

The instant Jesus finishes his sermon on the reign of God on earth, Mark shifts his narrative of God's reign in Jesus' person into high gear. We find ourselves blitzed by the ministry of Jesus Christ. In just sixty-three verses, Jesus manages to:

- call fishermen to a more distinguished vocation of fishing
- exorcise a foul spirit
- purge a virus from Simon's mother-in-law
- heal and exorcise an entire city (and more!)
- cleanse a leper's ulcers
- pardon a paralyzed man of his sin, then cure his paralysis
- hire Matthew from the tax collector's office, then seal the deal over dinner with the guild of sinners
- counter a professional critique of his leadership style
- entertain the clergy's negative assessment of his personal faith
- heal a congenital defect
- flee the crushing horde of Palestinian thrill seekers

Mark marches us relentlessly from scene to scene, pasting together a collage of images that boggle the church's imagination. The effect is a crescendoing wonderment over Jesus' power, authority, and person. The church is left reeling with the question of whether there's a force in creation, let alone Palestine, able to resist the rule of this one from Nazareth. Even the reader longs for a breather by the time we reach the middle of chapter 3.

Mark signals such a breather by bringing Jesus to a mountain. Throughout scripture, mountains provide pauses in the biblical narrative which are often filled with profound experiences of God. "The mountain setting," suggests Williamson (80), "may carry with it certain nuances of revelation and authority." The change of pace in Mark's storytelling is noticeable. We stand on the threshold of a momentous decision by Jesus Christ.

"He went up the mountain."

For the remainder of chapter 3, Mark will prod the church to reflect on the arresting character of Jesus' person. In two artistically interwoven scenes (vv. 21, 31–35 and vv. 22–30), Mark will create a medley of responses to Jesus that range from immediate obedience to absolute defilement. Mark wants us to feel the raw power of Jesus' person and to sense how impossible it was (and is) for anyone to respond to Jesus dispassionately. Jesus was so discriminating as to the inner person of those in his midst that they could become only *for* him or *against* him, but never indifferent toward him.

In this passage, Mark presents us with Jesus' demanding presence, not in the sense of strictness but of centeredness. Mark wants us to imagine that we cannot get near this one from Nazareth, for even a moment, and remain unchallenged in our identity. So Mark casts Jesus here as the one and only one with authority to tell us who we truly are and when we are lying about ourselves. With a transcendent power of discernment, Jesus identifies us and reidentifies us by the presence of his person and the wisdom of his words. Mark will have us know that in some mysterious but certain way Jesus Christ determines our destiny. Mark will warn in the gravest way that Jesus will not be deceived by us. But within this warning is also the promise of good news that Jesus involves us personally in the determination of our future. In short, here Mark communicates that Jesus Christ matters ultimately to everyone.

The Naming of the Twelve (3:13–19a)

While there is much within church history and everyday church life to impede us from finding ourselves in the original apostles, there can be no question here that what Jesus is doing on the mountain is digging the footings of the Christian church. Our elemental identity as God's Christian people—folk for whom the chief means of glorifying and enjoying God is following Jesus Christ—is tightly summarized here by Mark in Jesus' call to the Twelve.

English translations fail to bring out several artistic touches by Mark. The feel of the Greek runs like this:

> Jesus went up the mountain and called for him those whom he was wanting, and they left for him. And he fashioned twelve, whom he also named apostles, to be with him and to be apostled for proclamation and the removal of demons. So he fashioned the twelve.

What a moving image of the church this is! After a burst of strictly solitary ministry, Jesus Christ, Son of God, retreats and witnesses that God will reign on earth only by *sharing* that reign with ordinary folk. Once he personally sets the precedent for God's rule, Jesus *incorporates* God's rule in disciples. He thereby reveals one of the mysteries of God's sovereignty: the One who creates the world sustains the world *from within* the world. The world is a suitable place for the kingdom of God; humanity is a suitable embodiment for God; disciples are a suitable community for the rule of God.

"They were not wealthy; they had no special social position; they had no special education; they were not trained theologians; they were not high-ranking churchmen and ecclesiastics; they were twelve ordinary men."—Barclay, *The Gospel of Mark*, Daily Study Bible, 74.

In Mark's hands, Jesus' formation of the church is a profound affirmation of our humanity. Note how the church arises, is formed, and is sustained by Jesus' humanity. Mark carefully describes Jesus' call of the Twelve as Jesus' way of fulfilling his own inner yearning, "He called for him those whom he was wanting, and they left for him" (3:13). This is more than the formation of a team for ministry, this is Humanity needing humanity to redeem humanity. By its absence in this important moment, sin can be understood to be absolutely alien to human being.

What does Jesus do, once we respond to his call? Mark would say Jesus fashions and names us. He defines us. He lets us know who we most deeply are. With all due respect to the New Revised Standard Version of the New Testament, this act of Christ's is not an appointment, but a *definition;* it is not a labeling, but the *transference of new identity.* Using the common Greek verb for "doing" or "making" and the common Greek verb for "naming," Mark illustrates that the church is the artwork of Jesus in process. We are the ones fashioned and sent by Jesus Christ; our identity derives from our maker.

What is our purpose? Very simply, to be with Jesus and to be apostled by Jesus. The noun "apostle" in Greek (*apostolos*) also has a verbal form, "apostled" (*apostello*), both of which are employed here by Mark to get at the essence of the church. We are the "sent out ones" because we are "sent out"; we are sent out because that is who we are.

> "He called . . . they came . . . and he *made* them."—Williamson, *Mark,* Interpretation, 82.

Note, however, that as Jesus articulates it, the church's self-understanding derives from two foci: time and activity; or better, reflection and service; or even better, worship and mission. The "sent out ones" (apostles) understand who they are only as they are both *with* Jesus and *sent out* in Jesus' name. Only in the unity of time and activity, reflection and service, worship and mission can the church realize who it is and live up to its name.

If apostles are "apostled," what then is the purpose of "apostling"? With typical abruptness and brevity, Mark defines the mission of the church as twofold: to proclaim and to cast out. While Jesus does not define the content of the church's proclamation, clearly the word "proclaim" in Mark harks back to John and Jesus in chapter 1, where both were proclaiming good news. John proclaimed "an immersion into God's forgiveness" and Jesus likewise proclaimed "an immersion into God's reign on earth." Thus the apostles are sent out to proclaim gospel for the whole world; God has come in the person and presence of Jesus Christ to rule the world with messianic peace and justice. The earmark of the church's preaching is "Joy to the world, the Lord has come; let earth receive her King."

The church that merely proclaims, however, reduces itself to a choir and Jesus will have no choir for a church. So, he tells us, the church is to *act out* its proclamation. Not only are apostles sent to proclaim God's rule on earth, they are sent literally to *embody* God's rule. "Their ministry, like that of Jesus himself, will be to announce and in a sense to embody the presence of the Kingdom of God" (Williamson, 81). The most concise way for Mark to say this is to declare that the church is sent to cast out demons.

Demons, in Mark's worldview, represent pure opposition to God's person and purpose. Demons are aliens in God's kingdom and they must not be dealt with gently, but entirely eradicated. This is Mark's way of saying that the mission of apostles is to resist evil everywhere in the kingdom, at all times and in all forms. So intrinsic is this resistance to the church's identity that it became an essential element in the historic liturgy of Baptism in the form of the question: "Do you renounce evil?" Coming from Mark, that question to the candidate could read: "Will you cast out demons?"

> "From [the first followers'] close companionship with Jesus came the power to preach and to cast out demons; so today from our prayer life, Bible study, and Christian fellowship comes the power to serve in his name."—Williamson, *Mark*, Interpretation, 82.

So he fashioned the Twelve. And so, Jesus fashions us.

Jesus' True Kinship (3:19b–35)

After Jesus digs, names, and reidentifies the footings of the church, Mark tells us that he went "into a house" (3:19, literal trans.), probably that of friends or relatives alongside the Sea of Galilee. He was met by a disruptive, surging crowd that violated the sanctity of a simple Jewish supper. We are not told why the crowd wants to be near Jesus; we are only told of their intrusiveness. Something is dreadfully wrong. This is not a picture of evening table shalom, but instead a gathering of human craving. Clearly, the mountain retreat is over.

As Mark transitions us back to earth, note the way in which he sandwiches two scenes, one inside of another. In verse 21, Mark begins an encounter with Jesus' relatives, from which he breaks in verses 22–30 for an encounter with Jerusalem scribes, only to return in verses 31–35 to complete the encounter with relatives. Mark nests an encounter with scribes inside an encounter with kin. In doing so, Mark explores the variety of responses triggered by Jesus. Mark's aim is for the church to deeply explore what it means to be related to Jesus Christ.

> ### Ever hear of a Markan sandwich?
>
> Here and at other points in the Gospel (i.e., 5:21–43; 6:7–30; 11:12–25), Mark frames one story within another. This literary technique intends each of the two stories to enrich the understanding of the other.

How Are We and Jesus Related? (3:21)

Pop Christian culture has made it faddish to ask, "What would Jesus do?" In verse 21, by using some of Jesus' kin as straw figures, Mark tilts the question differently, "What would you do to Jesus?" There is no way to identify the motive of Jesus' people in verse 21; Mark leaves it deliciously ambiguous. All Mark suggests is that Jesus' own people are motivated in some way by the widespread belief that Jesus has lost his marbles, literally in the Greek, that he has "relocated outside himself." Jesus' people are motivated to restrain their crazy cousin. "Restrain" here is an aggressive Greek verb that can mean "seize," "grab," or "arrest." It is the word Mark later uses to describe the arrest of both John and Jesus. But we cannot know Mark's intent; we are left wondering whether Jesus' own people were trying to protect Jesus from the vicious rumors, whether they were in some way agreeing with the rumors and trying to straitjacket their cousin, or whether they were simply worried about the family name.

Does Our Relationship to Jesus Matter? (3:22–30)

At this point Mark pauses us in the question of family loyalty and takes us to a side stage for one of the most arduous passages in the New Testament. Interestingly enough, as Mark crafts the narrative, this is Jesus' first sustained teaching moment; it even includes Jesus' first parable.

The most important issue in understanding this encounter is to be sure of the structure of the argument. The second most important issue is to be sure we are able to see *ourselves* in the scribes' shoes, that is, to be sure we are not too easily concluding that we are "us" and the scribes are "them." We must steadfastly resist any reading that suggests that we are in any way above blasphemous behavior.

> **Who were the scribes?**
>
> A scribe originally was a secular official who functioned like a lawyer, interpreter, and copyist of the Torah. In time, scribes came to have more religious standing and were associated with the Pharisees.

First, let us grapple with the structure of the argument. Scribes, who are the bookish, technical, legal authorities for first-century Judaism, travel all the way from Jerusalem to the Sea of Galilee to diagnose Jesus, a distance of at least seventy miles. This is not an insignificant detail. Sometimes, when the stakes are high enough and our focus sharp enough, neither rain nor hail nor distance can stop us from our charge. The scribes come all this way to put forth their understanding of Jesus' alleged insanity: "Jesus is possessed by the lord of demons; that's why he can lord it over the demons!" (v. 22). Let us call this the diagnosis.

Jesus takes over from here and speaks for the rest of this encounter. Intriguingly, at this critical moment Jesus chooses to speak not straightforwardly, but parabolically. He will be using these scribes to reveal something that is not meant for them personally, but for those with eyes and ears for truth, the church. We will learn more about Mark's understanding of parables in chapter 4, but for now, let us accept Mark's difficult conviction that parables in Jesus' hand have a blinding as well as a revealing function. In other words, this is not so much an argument with evil scribes, but a teaching for the church about the nature and power of evil.

Let us continue to track the structure of the argument. If verse 22 is the scribes' diagnosis ("Jesus is possessed"), then verses 23–26 are Jesus' pronouncement that these professional interpreters have *mis*-diagnosed him ("If I'm possessed, Satan's schizophrenic"). Then in verse 27 Jesus provides the accurate diagnosis that the scribes failed to make ("I'm not possessed; I'm almighty, and I'm plundering the house of Evil"). Jesus then warns the church (not the scribes!) in verses 28–29 how catastrophic such a misdiagnosis turns out to be. There could be no clearer way for Jesus to communicate to the church that this behavior must never be indulged. As Williamson (84) puts it, "Jesus enjoys no kinship with Satan, but is his deadly enemy."

> "Mark's intention in these early verses is clear: Jesus is the agent of God's [kingdom] come to defeat the demonic powers opposed to God. Thus the exorcisms reveal the power of God's Holy Spirit at work in Jesus to defeat the unholy spirits."—Mitzi Minor, *The Spirituality of Mark: Responding to God* (Louisville, Ky.: Westminster John Knox Press, 1996), 78.

Jesus' warning in verses 28–29 might just be the most difficult passage in the Bible. The Greek text reads literally:

> Truly, all the sins of humanity will be forgiven, and as many blasphemies as you can count, but whoever blasphemes the Holy Spirit has no forgiveness into the ages, but is liable for an ages-long sin.

One of the reasons this text is so difficult is the church's historic abuse of it. Tearing this chilling verse from its context, the church has frequently wielded it as a weapon of coercion against nonbelievers or shrewdly offered it as an instrument of self-flagellation for believers. Jesus means neither. In fact, Jesus intends absolutely no *practical* use for this verse in the church's life. Instead, Jesus is affirming who he is—and that God is reigning in his person—in the clearest, most vivid, and most forcefully negative way imaginable. His interest here is not to forecast the eternal, personal destiny of the scribes, or anyone else for that matter, but to absolutely negate their absolutely negative assessment of him, so that the church will hear and embody his absolutely *positive* reality for the world.

Let us look at this from another, more theological angle. The glorious news for the world is that Jesus Christ, the Son of God, incarnates God. The scribes invert the reality of Jesus and declare instead that he incarnates Satan. The glorious news for the world is that Jesus Christ incarnates God's mercy. The scribes invert the reality of Jesus and declare instead that he incarnates God's mercilessness. The glorious news for the world is that Jesus Christ incarnates God's redeeming reign for the earth. The scribes invert the reality of Jesus and instead declare that he incarnates Satan's destructive attack on the earth. The scribes effectively look God in the eye and assert, "You are the perfect reciprocal of God."

The scribes commit the sin of absolute moral relativity; they collapse the moral universe in upon itself and thereby trap themselves within the black hole of moral blindness. If Jesus Christ is our glimpse of absolute hope, the scribes are our glimpse of absolute despair.

In other words, in misdiagnosing Jesus Christ the scribes are turning reality absolutely inside out, redefining absolute good (Jesus) as absolute evil (Beelzebul), looking at God eye-to-eye, if you will, and renaming God "Devil." Mark would have us know that engaging in this absolute inversion to any serious extent traps us in an inverted symbolic universe where everything appears as it is not.

This passage is Mark's peculiar way of affirming Jesus' identity as the Son of God in whose person God is reigning on

---

Want to Know More?

About demons? See Leland Ryken, James C. Wilhoit, and Tremper Longman III, eds., *Dictionary of Biblical Imagery* (Downers Grove, Ill.: InterVarsity Press, 1998), 202–4.

About exorcisms? See Richard P. McBrien, ed., *Encyclopedia of Catholicism* (San Francisco: Harper, 1995), 503–4.

About healing? See Donald K. McKim, *Encyclopedia of the Reformed Faith* (Louisville, Ky.: Westminster John Knox Press, 1992), 164–65; See also Zach Thomas, *Healing Touch: The Church's Forgotten Language* (Louisville, Ky.: Westminster John Knox Press, 1994).

About the unforgivable sin? See George Arthur Buttrick, ed., *The Interpreter's Dictionary of the Bible*, vol. R–Z (Nashville: Abingdon Press, 1962), 733–34.

earth. Mark wants the church to know beyond a shadow of doubt that our response to Jesus Christ matters in an ultimate way. Mark wants us to regard Jesus Christ with reverence, to stand in awe at his absolute power and utter humility, and to surrender ourselves to his Lordship. Williamson (86) confirms that Mark's intention in alluding to an "unforgivable sin" is to motivate the church's positive response to Jesus Christ:

> The sin is to recognize a supernatural power at work in Jesus and yet to call that power unclean or evil. The sin is unforgivable because it rejects the very agent of God's healing and forgiveness. . . . The text continues to function as a warning to all readers of the seriousness of our response to the One who confronts us here.

Another New Testament scholar, Paul Minear, helpfully describes the nature of this complex dilemma in God's universe. Try to appreciate the sense here in which God is not personally condemning us when we commit the unforgivable sin, but the way in which God's creation is designed to rectify our abusive behavior. A universe created with its own moral integrity and function is a very Jewish understanding of the world:

> We may not be far wrong if we say that to call the Holy Spirit "unclean" is to deny that the Holy Spirit has power to overcome the Devil. It is a flat denial that God can forgive sins. It is an absolute form of despair, for a person thereby rejects in advance the possibility that [people] can ever be freed from bondage to evil powers. In this despair, a person actually gives to Satan the status of Almighty Father. Such despair cannot be forgiven, because it bolts the only door by which forgiveness may enter. (Minear, 67)

In Williamson's (86) words, "Only those who set themselves against forgiveness are excluded from it."

To repeat, Mark is not warning the scribes about their personal future, so much as he is using the scribes to caution the church about the enormous significance of understanding clearly the person of Jesus Christ. Mark uses extreme terms not to frighten the church, but finally to reassure us that the person of Jesus Christ can be trusted absolutely. By warning us that tampering with Jesus Christ is life-threatening, Mark is persuading us that following Jesus Christ is life-giving. As the church comes down from the mountaintop behind Jesus, Mark wants there to remain not an iota of doubt in the church's faith that the spirit animating Jesus is the Spirit of the Holy One of Israel, which can be trusted in every wilderness of life and death.

Again, How Are We and Jesus Related? (3:31–35)

At this point, after he has sobered us about the seriousness of our response to Jesus Christ, Mark returns to the scene of Jesus' confrontation with his own people. Remember that Mark has nested the scribes inside an encounter with the folk who have grown up with Jesus and who should know him better than any. As we emerge from this encounter with the scribes, Mark sharpens the blurry focus on family with which the encounter began in verse 21 to "your mother and your brothers and sisters" in verse 32. We are left without any doubt whom Jesus will now confront.

The text immediately raises within us the question of preferential treatment. Will Jesus treat his own mother and siblings in any preferential way? What kind of response will Jesus' family display? Will they be permitted a more lenient form of discipleship?

Here Mark seems to be toying with us about the nature of a faithful response to Jesus. In one searing scene, Mark slays all affection, allegiance, and ceremony, and discloses that the journey behind Jesus will be no sentimental journey. On the one hand, Mark tells us that Jesus' mother and siblings arrive, stand outside, and call in to him from a distance, as if timid or reluctant or unable to find their way nearer. On the other hand, a crowd of *non*-relatives sits persistently around Jesus in what looks like an intimate circle. Instinctively, those within the circle alert Jesus to the presence of his beloved mother. To which Jesus replies with one of the more scandalizing questions in scripture: "Who is my mother?" We could accuse Jesus of sarcasm, were he not at every moment so centered in truth.

> "All Christians are called to be 'with Jesus' in this sense—not simply to learn *about* him but to learn *from* him how to live as signs of God's rule by acting compassionately and resisting evil."—Hare, *Mark*, Westminster Bible Companion, 48.

Jesus scandalizes us here because he dares to step outside the magic circle of preference. He dares to subvert the ways in which we settle into identities that cannot save us. He dares to insist that we become who we were intended to be and cease satisfying ourselves with identities that will not ultimately satisfy. Not only does Jesus reidentify fishermen and tax collectors, but he dares to reidentify his mother as crowd and the crowd as his mother! Jesus transgresses every sociocultural boundary! If ever there was a wake-up call for the church, Jesus provides it here: "The way to love me as my mother is to become fashioners of God's will with your lives."

With a dazzling touch of irony, Mark leaves us wondering whether our response to Jesus Christ is adequate. As this scene closes, we are left with the conviction that the way we posture ourselves toward Jesus determines how we are related to him. Those willing to sit near and listen hungrily for the will of God are those loving Jesus as only a mother loves her child. Those hailing Jesus from a distance, relying on familiarity for privilege, are those merely infatuated with Jesus' celebrity.

> "It came to the earliest church, and it still comes to the community of faith today, as a marching order, an invitation, and a promise. Whoever will hear *and do* this word may become the true relative of Jesus."
> Williamson,—*Mark,* Interpretation, 85.

Biology will not be equated with discipleship.

? Questions for Reflection

1. The writer of this study translates the verb in Mark 3:14–16 as "fashion" instead of "appoint." How does this difference in translation affect your understanding of these verses?
2. Consider the following quote from this unit: "Only in the unity of time and activity, reflection and service, worship and mission can the church realize who it is and live up to its name." What is the unity the writer is speaking about, and how can it be achieved?
3. Mark 3:21 and 31–35 are two of the scant references to the family of Jesus in the Gospel of Mark (see also 6:3; 15:40–16:1). Why do you suppose so little is said about the family of Jesus? Why would those references be vague and unflattering?
4. Mark 3:22–30 suggests an allusion to the story in Mark 5:1–20. Take a moment and read that story. What connection do you see between the two passages? What insight does either passage offer to the other?

Mark 4:1-34

The Mystery Discloses

The preceding passage pressed us to answer the question, How are we related to Jesus Christ? We recall that after an opening volley of solitary ministry, Jesus retreated to a mountaintop, called and fashioned twelve apostles, and yoked them to himself to share the Christian vocation of proclamation and exorcism.

At this mountain retreat, Jesus laid the foundation of the church and defined our vocation as the people who proclaim and embody the glorious news of God's reign on earth. With a few crisp words, Jesus identified us as the people immersed in God's triumph over evil (3:26–27). Though the church may have historically misconstrued the apostolic office as a hierarchy of the few, we dare to believe that Mark is calling us today to boldly assume the original vocation of the Twelve.

Having defined the church, Jesus then asked us the deeper question of what it means to be related to him. Through an encounter with religious professionals, nested within a family engagement, Mark characterized discipleship as a serious journey that ultimately determines human destiny, a journey on which there are no free rides. Mark concluded with a long, searching stare by Jesus and a piercing assertion that only those practicing a vocation pleasing to God can claim a meaningful relationship to Jesus Christ. Those who follow Jesus out of convenience are swept into the rubber-necking crowd, including even his own mother.

In the turbulent wake of chapter 3, Mark gives us chapter 4 as balm whenever we weary of our Christian vocation. A careful and comprehensive reading of this chapter will reward the church with nourishment and salve for the anxiety and ache of discipleship. Not only is this Jesus' first formal discourse in Mark's narrative, it is the longest teaching by Jesus in Mark's remembrance. Moreover, this is the first time we hear Jesus elaborate on his first sermon (in 1:14–15), about the coming of the kingdom of God to earth.

As we tackle this challenging passage, two critical issues surface. First, the passage must be handled as a unity, from start to finish. To separate any part of this passage from the whole is to compromise its capacity to speak. If a single piece of this passage "be washed away" by the reader, the chapter will be the less. Williamson (87) warns that only those who tenaciously keep the whole text in view will be rewarded with its meaning: "Attractively simple on the surface, the parabolic discourse of Jesus in Mark invites an ever-deepening dialogue through which we begin to perceive the promise of the kingdom and in which we encounter Jesus' repeated call to hear."

> "The art of the interpreter is to follow the lead of Scripture by taking up these stories in ever-new situations, allowing them the freedom to speak with fresh nuances while assuring continuity with their meaning in the canonical context."—Williamson, *Mark*, Interpretation, 89.

Mark himself pleads for the text's unity, urging us to read it as a unified word, by artistically packaging the passage in one complete seaside scene. In verse 1, "Jesus begins to teach beside the sea." He continues to do so until evening falls in verse 35, when he concludes, "Let us go across to the other side."

The second issue critical to releasing the power of this passage is to hear the words as words uttered by Jesus to his disciples but shaped by Mark to speak to you and me, disciples of today. In other words, while Mark narratively locates the scene of this fourth chapter in Jesus' day, Mark also intends that the scene speak to the church of Mark's day, and to generations thereafter.

The Ministry of the Disciples (4:1–34)

The whole point of this chapter is to empower us in our common vocation as witnesses to Jesus Christ. Mark's aim is to equip the church to scatter the good news of God's reign, then to scatter the good news again,

"Other seed fell into good soil and brought forth grain."

then to scatter it again and again and again—to sow gospel seed everywhere and be done, to let it go and to let God grow.

An admonition borrowed from the apostle Paul illustrates Mark's overriding concern: "Think of us this way, as *servants* of Christ and *stewards* of God's mysteries" (1 Cor. 4:1, NRSV, emphasis added). The interpretive key for this text is Mark's emphasis that the church must not aspire to be more than the servant of *an Other* and the steward of *an Other's* mysteries. Mark is trying to help us see that the power for this ministry is directly proportional to the humility of the minister; the more humble the sower, the more powerful the sowing. The more contentment the church finds as servant (rather than master) and as steward (rather than owner), the more effective the church's ministry.

The subtlety of this truth is elusive. Why is the modern church so unsatisfied with the humble role of sower? Why are we so easily infatuated with statistics, quantities, and results that mysteriously belong to the Grower alone?

Mark aims this teaching at a church like us, a church that is bone-weary because it is misconstruing its vocation. Mark writes for disciples who keep confusing the essential nature of service and stewardship. Mark writes for fatigued church workers who describe themselves as servants, but who continue to assume burdens that belong exclusively to their master; church workers who humbly name themselves stewards, but continue trying to bear mysteries that belong exclusively to the Creator. Mark has learned that such self-centeredness kills the church with exhaustion and stress. Mark knows that there is little that can be called good about a church trapped in the idolatry of self-importance. This is Mark's *magnum opus* on the sovereignty of God in our lives as disciples.

In the face of weariness, Williamson notes the motifs of encouragement and exhortation. Not only should we hear Jesus encouraging and exhorting his disciples, and not only should we hear Mark encouraging and exhorting members of the early church, but we too should hear encouragement and exhortation. "Encouragement is evident in the repeated contrast between small or discouraging beginnings and great or gratifying endings. Exhortation takes the form of repeated calls to hear and warnings about failure to hear rightly" (Williamson, 88).

This chapter weaves along a difficult way, so let us navigate the journey with the interpretive map that follows. Let us resist feeling that we have arrived until we have traversed the whole text. Then when we look back, we will understand better the journey's larger purpose.

An Interpretive Map for the Parables of the Kingdom

4:1–9   CROWD, the church should sow. Do not be misled into equating sowing and growing. Just sow. Understand this, if you are able.

4:10–12   DISCIPLES, *you* are the ones chosen to understand the mystery of God's kingdom. I will use parables to distinguish a church from the crowd, a remnant who will understand and co-labor with God's reign on earth.

4:13–20   DISCIPLES, don't you understand? Sow and leave the growing to God.

4:21–23   DISCIPLES, don't despair, sow! You're the ones who have been given the seed. Not sowing is like hiding the light of a lamp after you bring it into a room! Just bring it in and let it shine. Trust the Grower. Don't try to grow and sow, just concentrate on sowing! Do you understand?

4:24–25   DISCIPLES, don't despair, sow! Sowing is your purpose, your reason for being, your livelihood. It is by sowing that you *are*, so keep sowing. This mysterious seed can only become what it is if it leaves you. To hold on is to lose it. Sow!

4:26–29   DISCIPLES, don't despair, sow! The crop is not a matter of your technique and expertise! Just sow and sleep soundly. The growth will be automatic. Just sow and let go.

4:30–34   DISCIPLES, don't despair, sow! Don't worry about poor sowing. Even if you sow poorly, the crop is not in your hands. The kingdom of God does not abide by the standard rules of agriculture. The Grower can take anything you sow— *anything*—anywhere you sow it, anyway you sow it, and yield a bumper crop. So sow.

The Parable about Sowing the Gospel of the Kingdom of God (4:1–9)

To prevent us from downloading twentieth-century agriculture on a first-century agrarian image, Williamson (90) provides this fresh reminder of ancient farming:

The text takes us with a large crowd to the sloping hillside beside the lake where grain fields run down to the water. Fishermen and farmers can watch each other at their work, and scenes from the life of either would be familiar images to the other. All would know that farmers sowing a grain field in Galilee would first broadcast the seed and then plow it into the soil. Clumps of thistles, evident at the time of sowing, would disappear with the plowing, just as a wide shelf of rock would be revealed only when a plow scratched the thin surface above it. . . . Golden seed, rich with life, is broadcast from a pouch by a steady, rhythmic swing of the sower's arm, covering the whole area from which the sower already anticipates a crop. The seeds encounter various fates: Birds eat those that fall on the path which is not ploughed; rock leaves little room for roots in some parts of the field; thistle seeds, turned under here and there with those sown, spring up and choke the grain; and where the soil is good, the yield varies from stalk to stalk. Though the seeds meet different fates, the overall destiny of the scattered seed is fulfilled when the sower's vision becomes reality.

This helpful description enables us to see, perhaps for the first time, that in the ancient world virtually any yield at all meant that the sower's task and hope had been fulfilled. Our modern obsession with process and efficiency is foreign to this ancient concept of success. We must liberate ourselves from many otherwise valuable agricultural techniques in order to be able to scatter the seed of the gospel faithfully. The development of modern agriculture threatens to shatter Jesus' metaphor.

> "With Jesus there had come something absolutely new into the world. He was the embodiment of the Kingdom because His whole life was lived in complete accordance with the will of God."—William Barclay, *The Parables of Jesus* (Louisville, Ky.: Westminster John Knox Press, 1999), 36.

Remember, chapter 4 is not about the kingdom of corporate farming; it is about the reign of God on earth in the person of Jesus Christ. The plain fact is that God reigns by rules that only God understands and that are scandalously undecipherable by us. We may not be happy with this, but Mark is crystal clear that the rules of God rule.

The Purpose of Parables (4:10–12)

This passage is as troubling as the eternal sin passage in chapter 3. As we journey through chapter 4, we are tempted to stop at this particular scenic view and end the journey here. What Jesus says here tortures our modern sensibilities. Jesus declares that parables enable disciples to comprehend God's reign on earth and, at the same time, cloak God's reign in mystery for others.

Actually, Jesus says more than this. He makes it clear that God's reign on earth, for nondisciples, remains locked in parable to *prevent* them from comprehending God's reign, to *prevent* them from turning, and to *prevent* them from being released of guilt. There is no use trying to water down the scandal of Jesus' words. He clearly means that parables have a dual purpose, depending on whether one is a disciple or not, depending on whether one has been given the mystery of the kingdom of God or not. Parables either reveal or conceal, and Jesus uses them for both purposes, whether we like it or not.

> "To hear the word of and about Jesus, to believe it and act on it, this is the secret of the reign or rule of God in individuals, in the church, and in the world."—Williamson, *Mark*, Interpretation, 92–93.

However, the clarity of what Jesus is saying here is not the issue. What we must grapple with is Jesus' meaning in the context of his entire lecture in chapter 4. So let us make two moves to grasp Jesus' meaning. First, let us note that after verse 9, Jesus has pulled his disciples away from the very large seaside crowd to privately converse with them for the rest of the teaching. Let us also recall that, for Mark, *we* are the disciples, and that we are actually there in the boat with Jesus. We are his weary and confused followers. This strange saying is exclusively for the church.

Here we are in the boat, confused about Jesus' use of parables to convey God's reign. We are frustrated about the poor response to our sowing of the Gospel. We are even angry at our own lazy efforts. Perhaps we are quarreling with one another about evangelical technique. To us, Jesus sharply admonishes:

> You are not the crowd. You are my followers; they are my onlookers. You follow me because you've been given the gift of insight into who I am; the crowd simply looks on. For them, God's reign on earth through me remains mystery. The parables keep you and the crowd distinct from one another, for now. Since you are the sowers and not the growers, do not worry about where your seed grows and where it does not grow. Celebrate your job by *doing* your job. Whether or not what you sow ever takes root in the crowd is not your concern. Be grateful for your vocation and be grateful doing it.

The second move we must make to understand Jesus' meaning is a move back to the Old Testament. The scandalous part of this passage is a quote by Jesus of the prophet Isaiah. To grasp Jesus' intent, we must therefore wrestle first with Isaiah.

This text from Isaiah is one of the church's favorites, on which a number of hymns are based. Curiously, the church's hymns never address the part that Jesus quotes. In fact, the church almost always stops reading before we get to the part that interests Jesus! The text Jesus quotes is God's call of Isaiah to his prophetic ministry, Isaiah 6:1–13, and it should be read as a complete passage. We can be sure that when Jesus quoted part of this text, it was the *whole* passage that came flooding into the disciples' Jewish consciousness:

> [1]In the year that King Uzziah died, I saw the Lord sitting on a throne, high and lofty; and the hem of his robe filled the temple. [2]Seraphs were in attendance above him; each had six wings: with two they covered their faces, and with two they covered their feet, and with two they flew. [3]And one called to another and said: "Holy, holy, holy is the LORD of hosts; the whole earth is full of his glory." [4]The pivots on the thresholds shook at the voices of those who called, and the house filled with smoke. [5]And I said: "Woe is me! I am lost, for I am a man of unclean lips, and I live among a people of unclean lips; yet my eyes have seen the King, the LORD of hosts!" [6]Then one of the seraphs flew to me, holding a live coal that had been taken from the altar with a pair of tongs. [7]The seraph touched my mouth with it and said: "Now that this has touched your lips, your guilt has departed and your sin is blotted out." [8]Then I heard the voice of the Lord saying, "Whom shall I send, and who will go for us?" And I said, "Here am I; send me!" [9]And he said, "Go and say to this people: 'Keep listening, but do not comprehend; keep looking, but do not understand.' [10]Make the mind of this people dull, and stop their ears, and shut their eyes, so that they may not look with their eyes, and listen with their ears, and comprehend with their minds, and turn and be healed." [11]Then I said, "How long, O Lord?" And he said: "Until cities lie waste without inhabitant, and houses without people, and the land is utterly desolate; [12]until the LORD sends everyone far away, and vast is the emptiness in the midst of the land. [13]Even if a tenth part remain in it, it will be burned again, like a terebinth or an oak whose stump remains standing when it is felled." The holy seed is its stump. (Isa. 1:1–13, NRSV)

Jesus is saying to the disciples that his calling is similar to Isaiah's terrifying call. Jesus is associating himself with Isaiah and telling the disciples that he, like Isaiah, is called by God to "make the mind of this people dull, and stop their ears, and shut their eyes, so that they may not look with their eyes, and listen with their ears, and comprehend with their minds, and turn and be healed" (Isa. 6:9–10, NRSV).

How painful this is to hear! We immediately resist its clear meaning. We combat the obvious sense of Jesus' words, until we read on and discover that Isaiah was called to do this only until the land was left with a holy seed that would sprout anew into a stump. Actually, the Greek Bible that Jesus probably quoted from is considerably different here than the Hebrew Bible that we read today (though the Hebrew also supports such a reading). The conclusion of the passage quoted by Jesus, Isaiah 6:12–13, in the Greek Bible reads as follows:

> [12]And after this God will remove the people far off, and the ones who will be left upon the earth will be multiplied. [13]And yet upon the earth is the tenth, and again it will be as a trophy of war, as a turpentine tree, and as an acorn when it fell from its casing.

"The tenth . . . will be . . . as an acorn when it fell from its casing." Here we meet Israel's theology of a remnant, the conviction that so long as a remnant of God's chosen people survives, God has been faithful to the everlasting covenant with Israel. Israel's remnant theology is even more profound in the Greek translation and helps us glimpse Jesus' meaning in this difficult saying. The call of Jesus has to do with winning from the battle a small fraction of loyalists who retain the germinating capacity of an acorn loosed from its outer shell.

Jesus is telling the disciples that the function of parables is to assure that a remnant will survive who will continue to sow the gospel of God's kingdom come. What makes this idea of a remnant palatable to us as an act of God's mercy is the belief by the Hebrew people (evident throughout the Old Testament) that even if a tiny fraction of Israel survives, *all of Israel survives with them.* The ancient Hebrew people, the Jews of Jesus' day, and even contemporary Jews embody this corporate personality in a way that seems alien to individualistic Americans who define freedom as an issue of personal rights.

Verses 10–12 of Mark 4, strange as they sound at first, thus provide the interpretive key for the entire passage. Jesus is attempting to encourage and exhort the church in its mission to sow the news of God's reign on earth. The church has met resistance from without and from within, and wilts from the pressure. Jesus draws on Isaiah to make it clear that with the use of parabolic teaching he is circumscribing the church (those who have been given the mystery of the kingdom of God), and identifying them as the remnant of humanity upon whom the survival of humanity depends. Jesus encourages the church in its identity as sower and exhorts the church to steadfastly continue with its mission of sowing. Let us now try to hear this complex passage in full, having untied its tightest knot.

Help with Interpretation (4:13–20)

Perhaps Jesus is gesturing toward different groups in the crowd on the seashore as he explains the parable of the sower; perhaps he is scattering handfuls of seed as he speaks. What we have here is a rare occurrence in the Gospels: a phrase-by-phrase, literal explanation of the meaning of a teaching by Jesus. The explanation is so literal, it is almost embarrassing. This unusual moment in Jesus' ministry is Mark's way of signaling a teaching of central importance to the church.

Verses 13–20 are one of the primary reasons for our confidence that Mark is taking a scene from the life of Jesus and reworking it for congregations under his care. In few other places in the Gospels does the life and struggle of the early church peek through as it does here. We can hear Mark's sermon to his weary congregation, urging them to keep on keeping on with the sowing. We can hear Mark exhorting them not to despair that Satan rushes in and steals their seed from potential converts. We can hear him lamenting over those converts who at first appear to understand the glory of God's reign on earth but who are unable to persevere as the storm of hostility strengthens. We can hear Mark cite the power of day-to-day pressures, material prosperity, and lust for status that chokes from human consciousness the sense that God rules the world.

But we can also hear Mark's joy over those few who are able to hear what the church is sowing, accept it, and bear fruit beyond anyone's imagination. These few are exactly why you cannot give up, Mark exhorts. They alone are worth your life.

> "Really to hear the gospel is to act upon it."—Williamson, *Mark*, Interpretation, 95.

Following this sermon, Mark juxtaposes four dimensions of sowing: its worth, its value, its autonomy, and its open-endedness. The ministry of the gospel is worthwhile, intrinsically valuable, independently fruitful, and totally unpredictable. Mark leaves no reason to cease sowing the seeds of God's reign here on earth.

The Worth of This Ministry of Sowing to God (4:21–23)

Here Jesus asks a razor-edged, rhetorical question: Should you conceal what cannot by nature be concealed? The image of a lamp beneath a basket, or table perhaps, even connotes danger: Should you conceal what is dangerous for you to conceal?

Absolutely not.

Jesus addresses the disciples' complaint that what they've been given is a mystery and has been challenging to convey:

> Jesus, how on earth are we to communicate a mystery like the reign of God on earth? There's too much hiddenness and secrecy! We proclaim to the crowd exactly what you've instructed us to proclaim—that "the reign of God has drawn near"—but folks don't get it! We're tired and frustrated and confused. We want to stop.

Such is the struggle of evangelism. To which Jesus addresses this remarkable statement about the sovereignty of God. Jesus declares that God's rule on earth is hidden (*kryptos*—from which derives our "cryptic") and secret (*apokryphos*—from which derives our "apocryphal") *in order to* make it visible. In other words, the concealed character of God's reign on earth has the larger purpose of becoming unconcealed. Jesus encourages the church not to gauge the worth of its mission on the immediate visibility or decipherability of God's reign. For now, the church is to confidently proclaim and embody what is hidden and secret to everyone else, trusting that one day all will be visible to all. "Though it may seem unexplainable," Jesus admonishes, "it is critical that you continue to sow."

> "Much that is crucial to the success or failure is beyond the control of the sower. Sowing is inevitably done in trust and hope, and the outcome is never sure."—R. David Kaylor, *Jesus the Prophet: His Vision of the Kingdom on Earth* (Louisville, Ky.: Westminster John Knox Press, 1994), 141.

Earlier Jesus had described the disciples' gift as the "mystery" of God's reign (v. 11), a word the New Revised Standard Version translates as "secret," even though "mystery" is how the Greek word (*mysterion*) transcribes into English. This is Mark's only use of the word "mystery" in his Gospel, as "hidden" and "secret" are his only uses of those respective words. These singular occurrences of three words bearing similar connotation signal the importance of this text.

What we have here is a key to the enigmatic behavior of Jesus in Mark's Gospel that we have come to describe as messianic secrecy, Jesus' reluctance to permit the immediate and unrestrained proclamation of him by recipients of his mercy. Mark appreciates more sharply than anyone that the kingdom of God is a secret hidden within God; it belongs to God to give, not to humanity. Mark appreciates that God's reign is God's alone to disclose and decipher, not humanity's; that God alone will unveil the mystery in God's own timing. We may proclaim the gospel of God's reign, but once the proclamation leaves our lips, it is as seed that leaves the sower's hand.

The Value of the Sowing to Disciples (4:24–25)

Jesus now addresses another anxiety within the disciples, their concern about the value of the gospel ministry to themselves. This is not so much a question of whether God's reign is worth proclaiming from God's point of view, but whether the proclamation of God's reign is intrinsically valuable to the proclaimer. Perhaps the question Jesus targets here runs something like this, "We understand the worth of ministry for its own sake, but what's the use of it for us?"

Interestingly, the fundamental struggles within the church today are not essentially different than the fundamental struggles within Mark's church, and the fundamental struggles within Mark's church were not essentially different from the fundamental struggles within the congregation of Jesus' disciples.

To the self-concern of the church, Jesus says, "Beware mistaking what has been given to you as if it is a commodity that now requires your decision to sell or not to sell. You simply do not have any decision to make." Here Jesus warns the church against trying to possess that which by nature cannot be possessed. He characterizes Christian ministry as a dynamic reality that has determinative power for the church. Insofar as we minister, we will minister more and more effec-

Want to Know More?

About parables? See James L. Bailey and Lyle D. Vander Broek, *Literary Forms in the New Testament: A Handbook* (Louisville, Ky.: Westminster John Knox Press, 1992), 105–14.

About being blind to the message of the parables? See Robert H. Stein, *An Introduction to the Parables of Jesus* (Philadelphia: Westminster Press, 1981), 27–35.

About agriculture in Palestine? See Paul J. Achtemeier, ed., *Harper's Bible Dictionary* (San Francisco: Harper & Row, 1985), 303–4.

tively; insofar as we withhold, we will lose even the capacity we had. The news of the kingdom of God on earth is a seed that cannot be stored; it must be sown.

Jesus wants the church to know of this dynamic quality about Christian identity. Only by sowing the gospel do we learn who-we-are and receive enough more of who-we-are to continue sowing. Jesus carefully uses passive verbs to clarify once again that this capacity for discipleship is not self-generated capacity, but capacity that is given (or taken!) by One who is beyond all selves. The church that maintains the will to sow receives the capacity; the church that relinquishes the will has the capacity taken away. This should not be viewed as a vindictive act by God, but as the natural, give-and-take reality of "a power whose life-giving potential is irrepressible" (Williamson, 91). In the words of the missionary Jim Elliot, who died by the spear of the Auca Indians to whom he was ministering in Ecuador, "He is no fool who gives what he cannot keep to gain what he cannot lose" (Elliot, 15).

The Autonomy of the Ministry of Sowing (4:26–29)

Two further, more practical dimensions of Christian ministry remain to be clarified and asserted by Jesus for the sake of the disciples: the role of the sower after the sowing and the predictability of the results. In both these concluding paragraphs, Jesus is explicitly clear that the kingdom of God is his subject, using the phrase each time. Having affirmed that the kingdom of God in Christ is of ultimate worth to God and value to the church, Jesus provides two parables of practical reassurance.

With a sense of humor, Jesus reminds the disciples that the One waiting to grow what they sow is so capable that all they need to do after they throw the gospel on the ground is to go to bed! "While you sleep, the gospel will grow," Jesus says with a glimmer in his eye, "and you'll never figure it out!" Stop calculating, stop worrying about design and strategy, stop trying to crunch results. Scatter what you have and hit the sack.

To drive his point home, Jesus emphasizes

the autonomy of the growing process, actually using the word from which we get our English "automatic." He describes the process as effortless: "Of itself [*automatos*], the earth produces." While you sleep—absolutely independent of you—the seed of God's kingdom germinates and grows to maturity. You see to the sowing and God sees to the growing. When the gospel is sown and left in the hands of God, its power for life is irrepressible.

The Open-Endedness of Sowing (4:30–32)

Jesus' last word in this lecture is meant to dispel regret and guilt over every perceived failure of ministry. Indeed, Jesus contends that the presence of regret or guilt indicates that the church has become church-centered. The mere presence of regret is an indicator of self-reliance.

Here Jesus aptly summarizes the entire passage, admonishing that the church which understands the worth of the gospel ministry and reposes the ministry completely in God's hands will be the church that does not concern itself with things beyond its control. This church should gladly broadcast whatever seed it has at the moment, even if it is seed scarcely visible to the naked eye. This church should not be obsessed with results but rest soundly in the sovereignty of God. If mistakes are made, if neglect occasionally creeps in, if less than 100 percent is given, this church should awaken afresh, mount up with wings, and soar to sow some more.

Jesus forcefully communicates that we are servants of *an Other* and stewards of mysteries that belong entirely to *an Other*. So capable is this Other of reigning here on earth that even the tiniest and most insignificant word of hope cast recklessly by the church can be grown into a sprawling refuge of gospel shade for the many.

Jesus admonishes the church to retain its humble station, to cast generously whatever of the gospel the church has to cast in the moment, and to rest from its labor in the full assurance that the seed which has been mysteriously given has now been rightfully returned to the Giver.

? Questions for Reflection

1. We might summarize this unit as an exhortation to the faithful to sow without ceasing, and let the results be God's alone. Too easily

in our lives, we become "results conscious." Why is that? What alternative do these verses offer as assistance?

2. These stories of planting and sowing describe scenes of significant risk which may be lost in our day. Read them again. In one, three quarters of the investment is lost due to factors completely out of the control of the sower. Another of the stories concedes that the seed grows "he does not know how" and "the earth produces of itself." What are situations that seem out of control or pose risk today? Do these parables speak to all risky situations, or only to the ministries of the church?

3. What do these verses say about Jesus' purpose in telling parables? What is your understanding of these verses?

4. Using a concordance, look up the word "shade" and check the references. What are the images of shade in the Bible? How do those images affect your understanding of verses 30–32?

The Mystery Calms

Jesus sails from his stormy lecture on discipleship (4:1–34) straight into another storm, and one of the church's most beloved stories. We have even adopted this story as a symbol for the church: a ship with a cross for a mast, heaving through the gale of life.

Mark makes it clear that this is not just another afternoon squall on the Sea of Galilee, but a whirlwind from hell which might drown the church in a watery abyss. Mark paints this scene, captured so powerfully by Rembrandt van Rijn in his painting *The Storm on the Sea of Galilee,* to typify the mighty challenges confronting Christian community throughout the centuries. So far in Mark's narrative, the disciples have heard their calling. Now they must know the gates of hell cannot prevail against them.

We are about to examine the nature of Jesus' power. For the next fifty verses, we will walk with the Son of God straight into the eye of four storms within human existence.

The Storm on the Sea of Galilee, by
Rembrandt Harmensz van Rijn.

Thus far, we have encountered many miraculous deeds, including the expulsion of a convulsing spirit (1:21–28), the healing of leprosy (1:40–45), the curing of paralysis (2:1–12), and the restoration of a congenitally malformed hand (3:1–6). Up to this point, however, Jesus' deeds have only piqued our curiosity about his identity. Until now the mighty deeds have been sideshows along the way to Jesus' person.

Now, beginning with a storm on the sea, Mark moves Jesus' miraculous power from side to center stage. No longer interested in indirectly prodding our curiosity about Jesus, Mark wishes to dazzle the church with Jesus' sheer might—to leave us breathless, awed, and without excuse in the courage of our discipleship.

With these stories, Mark converges the power of Jesus with his baptismal identity as God's beloved Son. No longer the means to other revelation, Jesus' acts in chapter 4 become *ends* in and of themselves, *the* revelation. In this breathtaking narrative, *who Jesus is* can only be fully grasped in *what Jesus does*. When this narrative is complete, the miracle-working power of Jesus will stand apart from the everyday magic of all other powerful persons in the ancient world.

We set sail into Jesus' person on the Sea of Galilee as the powers of the abyss pound over the gunwale of our boat. We make it to the eastern shore, to the eerie country of the Gerasenes, where a soul fouled by evil lunges at our faith. We are forced back to the western shore, where a street woman stalks us. Finally, the death of a twelve-year-old child threatens to steal the last breath of our discipleship. Miraculously, we survive. And Jesus is made known to us as Lord over chaos, the living embodiment of Sabbath calm.

Mark juxtaposes these mighty deeds to give them cumulative impact. He tumbles them together in the church's imagination as an incomparable witness that creation harbors no chaos strong enough to overcome the reordering power of the Creator. As it was in the beginning, it is now for the church: the formlessness and void of our lives, the watery madness and demonic estrangement, are, to God, the clay of creation.

In these incidents, Mark highlights the fragility of life and provokes us to ponder the vicissitudes of human existence—accidents of nature, personified evil, mental illness, chronic bodily dysfunction, societal ostracism, premature death, the loss of a future. Mark forces the question: Are you convinced yet, that neither death, nor life, nor angels, nor rulers, nor things present, nor things to come, nor powers, nor height, nor depth, nor any other chaos threatening creation can separate you from God? Or have you still no faith?

With four magnificent acts of creation out of chaos, Mark delivers relief to the church, relief that restores our confidence as disciples.

In days of crisis and opportunity in the church, may we find ourselves on the banks of this shore time and again.

The Calming of the Storm (4:35–41)

There was no more effective way for Mark to communicate Jesus' mastery over chaos than to begin with water. The early church was the heir of a Hebrew cosmology in which the Creator, the Lord God, was constantly battling to hold the waters of chaos away from the dry, ordered creation. Water held unfathomable mystery for the ancients; it was forceful and unknowable and entirely unpredictable. This is why the story of the stilling of the winds and waves of the Galilean sea is paradigmatic for Jesus' Lordship. "The stilling of the storm continues to reassure the church in every time of persecution and distress that Jesus Christ is Lord, that he is ruler of nature *and* history, and that he is present with his disciples in their anxiety" (Williamson, 102).

Whenever chaos intruded into human existence in the ancient world, it was a reminder to the Hebrews of the awesome primordial power exerted by God in creation:

> By the word of the LORD the heavens were made, and all their host by the breath of his mouth. He gathered the waters of the sea as in a bottle; he put the deeps in storehouses. Let all the earth fear the LORD; let all the inhabitants of the world stand in awe of him. For he spoke, and it came to be; he commanded, and it stood firm. (Ps. 33:6–9, NRSV)

Indeed, Isaiah suggests that God's *competence* as Lord over creation could essentially be measured by God's ability to rule chaos:

> For thus says the LORD, who created the heavens (he is God!), who formed the earth and made it (he established it; he did not create it a chaos, he formed it to be inhabited!): I am the LORD, and there is no other. (Isa. 45:18, NRSV)

Disorder in human life, particularly when it tore at the fabric of Israel's covenantal relationship, provided the occasion for Israel's boldest praying. In these moments of covenantal disquiet, Israel imaged itself as trapped by wind and water:

> Save me, O God, for the waters have come up to my neck. I sink in deep mire, where there is no foothold; I have come into deep waters,

and the flood sweeps over me. I am weary with my crying; my throat is parched. My eyes grow dim with waiting for my God. . . . O God, in the abundance of your steadfast love, answer me. With your faithful help rescue me from sinking in the mire; let me be delivered from my enemies and from the deep waters. Do not let the flood sweep over me, or the deep swallow me up, or the Pit close its mouth over me. (Ps. 69:1–3, 13–15, NRSV)

In order to grasp the power of this favorite story of the stilling of the storm, we must discard worn interpretations and reconsider the three central realities of the story: (1) the storm; (2) the sleep of Jesus; and (3) Jesus' interaction with the disciples.

First, let us reconsider the storm. The church has been tempted to read this as an abrupt but ordinary weather system over the Sea of Galilee and then to subtly treat Jesus as an omniscient meteorologist who sleeps smugly in the knowledge that it will blow over in time. However, Mark clues us that this is not about the weather at all. By using the word that had been made famous by God's reply to Job, Mark reveals that there is a larger, theological purpose. In Job 38:1 and 40:6, God finally responds to Job out of the "whirlwind," a Hebrew word that best translates as some form of savage, cosmic tempest. This word in the Greek Old Testament (the Septuagint) is exactly the word Mark chooses to describe the gale that frenzies the Sea of Galilee. Moreover, he dares to amplify it with an adjective: this is a *mega* whirlwind!

Straightaway we know this is about more than wind and water. This is an awful, primordial eruption of evil and we are smack in the middle of it. Mark will not allow us to attenuate its force; he will not permit us to sidestep the concrete threat to Jesus and his disciples. With vivid narrative, he imprisons us in that fateful vessel: "the waves beat into the boat, so that the boat was already being swamped" (Mark 4:37, NRSV).

Secondly, we must reconsider the sleep of Jesus. Here, more than at any other point in this short story, the church is inclined to flatten the text. We flatten it because the whole picture of the Lord Jesus asleep in the midst of our crisis is imaginatively unmanageable. We are unequipped to handle the simple reality of Jesus' sleep. Either we patronize Jesus for such weariness ("What kind of Lord is it who succumbs to fatigue at such a moment?") or we castigate him for toying with our faith ("What kind of Lord is it who tests and teases when we are so vulnerable?"). Both readings miss the point of the story, however, and subvert its power.

The only adequate explanation for Jesus' sleep is that he is utterly fearless over the prospect of dying. Jesus can sleep at this moment because he suffers no anxiety over death. Jesus can sleep in the back of a thrashing, swamped, doomed fishing vessel because he sleeps the sleep of a faithful Jew who entrusts his future entirely to the Lord of his past, "I lie down and sleep; I wake again, for the LORD sustains me. I am not afraid of ten thousands of people who have set themselves against me all around" (Ps. 3:5–6, NRSV). Jesus, Son of God, sleeps neither in fatigue nor in neglect nor in arrogant presumption about his power over nature; he sleeps in covenantal confidence that the existence of everyone in that boat is safely enfolded in the hands of Israel's God, who will be true to the covenant even in death.

Thirdly, we must reconsider Jesus and the disciples. Understanding first that the storm is truly a killer, and secondly that Jesus sleeps confident in the midst of dying, we must evaluate anew Jesus' interaction with the disciples. A killer storm has come out of nowhere and the disciples are tightly in its grip. Mark does not exaggerate; the disciples are being swallowed into the abyss and they know it. Their cry is the panicked cry of the "fight or flight" reflex: "Teacher, you are not concerned that we are being destroyed!"

Jesus awakes and asserts his authority over the chaos, commanding it as one would command a loud and unruly dog: "Be dumb! Be muzzled!" He exhibits no charity: "Sit down and shut up!" Then Jesus turns to the disciples and asks a pointed, double question that we must get right: "Why are you timid, not yet trusting?" This is not a question about fear (Jesus avoids using the common word for fear), this is a question about *confidence.* Jesus is not being sarcastic or condescending; he is genuinely concerned about the disciples' incapacity to trust God at such a critical moment.

> "The word to the storm becomes for us a voice from the whirlwind."—Williamson, *Mark,* Interpretation, 103.

Ironically, Mark tells us that fear (the Greek word is *phobos*) enters the disciples only at this point, after all is quiet, *in response to* Jesus' calming deed and word! Sure, the disciples are frightened in the midst of their encounter with chaos, but Mark notes very shrewdly that it is during their encounter with Jesus that they become *greatly fearful.* Not only was he able to sleep into death, but he expected them to sleep too!

In that moment, even chaos seems calm compared to the power of Jesus' person! The disciples lack all cognitive capacity for this startling revelation and they want to flee in terror: "Who is this here beside us

48

in the boat, to whom *chaos* bows? 'When the waters saw you, O God, when the waters saw you, they were afraid; the very deep trembled' " (Ps. 77:16, NRSV). "My God, what kind of mistake have we made?"

> "[This story] affirms that the Creator of this vast universe, the power behind the 'Big Bang,' is not to be conceived of as a watch-maker who wound up the universe and abandoned it to run on its own, but as involved and interactive."—Hare, *Mark*, Westminster Bible Companion, 62.

The Calming of Past, Present, and Future (5:1–43)

We now turn to three concrete manifestations of this authority in human life. Each of these three miracles deals with a facet of human experience that can be related to time. As Jesus encounters the Gerasene demoniac, he calms the chaos of the past; in his encounter with chronic illness in the untouchable woman, Jesus calms the chaos of the present; and in his encounter with death in Jairus' daughter, Jesus calms the chaos of the future. In every sphere of human existence, Jesus reigns over disorder.

The Calming of the Past (5:1–20)

This encounter with the man-out-of-the-tombs is a horrific scene of evil. It is odd that this story sometimes serves as the butt of humor in the church. What we have here is anything but humorous, and the question must be pressed whether or not we have lost (abdicated) our capacity (responsibility) to name evil.

This is a rich passage with much to occupy our imagination. However, we are primarily interested in coming to grips with Mark's testimony of Jesus' Lordship over the way in which the chaos of our past can haunt human existence in the present. So let us concentrate our interpretive energy on two areas, the nature of the demoniac's dilemma and the nature of the neighborhood's response.

Remember that the voyage we finish here on the other side of the sea is the same voyage in which we have just experienced Jesus' incredible power over wind and water. Such a voyage would have covered six to seven miles and lasted a daytime. The great fear that filled us on the sea lingers as we beach the boat on the Gentile eastern shore.

As soon as Jesus' foot touches the sand, he is accosted by a raving madman emerging from the tombs. The horror of our situation immediately dawns; we have landed not only in Gentile territory for the first time in the Gospel, but we have landed amidst the tombs where the Gentile dead are laid—and one of their living dead is attacking us! It's a gruesome predicament in which no right-minded Jew would be found. Ancient Israel viewed Gentile territory with disdain, as instructed by the Lord: "The land that you are entering to possess is a land unclean with the pollutions of the peoples of the lands, with their abominations. They have filled it from end to end with their uncleanness" (Ezra 9:11, NRSV). Moreover, ancient Israel maintained a perpetual statute prohibiting contact with a human corpse or human grave. This statute even included alien Gentiles residing among the Jews and was accompanied by an elaborate ritual of cleansing after seven days of uncleanness (see Num. 19:10b-22).

Mark does not soften the ghoulishness of this scene. In fact, he seems to go out of his way to paint it with dread: this miserable Gerasene has become the unclean of the unclean; he lives where the unclean decompose; he is so violent he can shatter the iron—and iron will—of an entire region. He roams freely night and day like a crazed, rabid wolf, biting himself and howling his misery. He is pathetic. The reader will be hard-pressed to find a scene more shuddering than this in the whole canon of scripture.

While Mark never informs us as to whether Jesus has a specific reason for crossing into this forbidden territory, a careful reading will reveal that, even in this abrupt and unexpected encounter, Jesus holds true to his larger purpose of ruling evil. In verse 8 we learn that the instant he discerns this concentrated evil "from a distance," Jesus seizes the initiative, speaks first, and *continues* to speak until the demon responds. The tenor of Jesus' command is no less aggressive with the whirlwind of the Gerasene's mind than it was with the wind and water: "Come out of the man, you unclean spirit! Come out! Get lost, you foulness! I command you, be dumb, be muzzled, be gone!"

> "There is no human disorder, anywhere, anytime, that Jesus cannot heal."—Williamson, *Mark*, Interpretation, 104.

Further careful reading reveals the horror: evil has completely enmeshed itself with the Gerasene's self. He is no longer an individuated human being; he has been taken over by another; every contour of his identity has been occupied by evil. The pitiful man is a mere shell inhabited by evil. As this shell—this monstrosity—runs, bows, shouts, and pleas, the reader confusedly flips back and forth from human to demon, ever uncertain which is which. Mark climaxes the horror when Jesus searches for its name. We are speechless as the demon replicates itself in mid-sentence, multiplying from singular to plural: "*MY* name is Legion; for *WE* are many!" Mark wants the church inside this nightmarish encounter, experiencing evil as Jesus experienced it, face-to-face. Mark wants the church to be in touch with the inner character and essential nature of evil, its "multiplicity, disorder, [and] violence" (Williamson, 105).

The exorcism is well-known and broadly parodied. Mostly, the church has been distracted with questions: Why does Jesus show mercy to the legion and give them what they want (permission)? Doesn't Jesus care about the two thousand pigs? Or the swineherds? Or the region's principal economy? Williamson's (104) insight here is sufficient: "Jesus accedes to [the demons'] requests, but in doing so he effectively sends the demons back to their place: the primeval abyss, the depths of

the sea. . . . Jesus accepts their proposal but defeats their purpose. His authority prevails." The scene tells all: pig piling upon pig, thrashing, screaming, choking to death on the muddy waters of the Sea of Galilee. And the madman has been given back himself, as it was in the beginning.

Now let us consider the day in the neighborhood. As Mark relays, the swineherds flee the scene and tell all. As the neighborhood collects in the becalmed graveyard, they experience the same emotion as the disciples in the becalmed sea: fear (*phobos*). As with the disciples, outer calm does not necessarily beget inner calm. Fear floods the neighborhood and they beg Jesus to remove himself. He obliges their wish. But before the scene closes, Mark touches us in verses 18–19 with the picture of absolute conversion: legion evil transformed into discipleship, a wickedly dissociative personality fashioned into an apostle, a howler of self-mutilation remade into a proclaimer of the reign of God on earth in Jesus Christ—the first Gentile mission in the Gospel of Mark. We weep as we overhear the healed man pleading to ride in the boat beside his hero.

In this scene Mark deftly paints the power of Jesus to calm the chaos of our past. Everyone in this scene (except Jesus) begs for things to remain as they are. Nobody wants the status quo to be disrupted. The Gerasene's neighborhood has devolved into a "well-adjusted" system where the forces of evil conveniently nullify the forces of good. The harmony of a village depends on the torment of an individual. Shalom no longer includes everyone, but has been reduced to a reality for the privileged.

Jesus disembarks into this codependency and fractures it forever. He discloses that God will reign over individual and village alike, that there is no such reality as the shalom of one without the other. No matter the degree of disorder, neither villager nor village need be bound by the way things have been. "This is the way it's always been" is not the Son of the Most High God's understanding of freedom.

The Calming of the Present (5:25–34)

Mark moves us back to the near side of the Sea of Galilee for two further encounters with human beings adrift in storms of chaos. Mark begins with the question of our future, phrased in the form of Jairus' young daughter who is perched at the threshold of death. The urgency of this need is immediate. All Jesus need do is lay hands on the girl and she will live. All Jesus need do is hurry and get there. It's that simple: "Come and touch her so that she may be saved" (v. 23).

"For all his power, Jesus does not force himself on those who fear the cost of his healing more than they love the cure . . . or the healer."—Williamson, *Mark*, Interpretation, 106.

But no, for Jesus the chaos that must be dealt with is the chaos at hand. All it takes is a victim's present touch to divert Jesus from the race to save Jairus' future. In his effort to provide willful healing, healing is provided even apart from his will. Mark portrays Jesus' reign over chaos as abundant and available.

As we read this unique account of an unwilled but conscious release of Jesus' power, we must grapple with the scandal of its availability. As the large crowd presses in on Jesus and his disciples, there is among them one whose desperation cuts a swath to Jesus' side. Ironically, this one is an untouchable in the culture's view: she is a woman; she is a nameless woman; she is a bleeding, nameless woman; she is a notorious, bleeding, nameless woman; she is a broke, notorious, bleeding, nameless woman. She is so marginalized from without and from within that she cannot face even her savior, but must creep up behind. We can be sure she is outcast. We can be sure she knows she is outcast. We can be sure society makes sure she knows. We can be sure this human being's worth is defined entirely by her present calamity. Every possibility for newness is sucked into the moral vortex of her body's chaos.

Except this one, last determination: "If I just touch his clothes, I will be saved" (v. 28). For all we know, she has heard of Jesus as we come to hear of television healers, with suspicion, skepticism, and scorn. Nevertheless, she has heard. So, with nothing to lose but her pain, she leans into what she has heard. She trusts.

Immediately, she is healed. Simultaneously, both she and Jesus recognize the energy of healing. As Mark puts it, the woman recognizes the permanency of her new health and Jesus recognizes that someone near him has received his ordering power. Jesus turns and begins urgently asking, "Who? Who? Who touched my clothes?" (v. 30).

The moment Jesus senses the healing is the moment he must stop everything else, even his journey to the synagogue leader's dying daughter. No wonder Mark nests this story within the story of Jesus' victory over death. A random healing must not remain random but must immediately find its completion in salvation. Therefore Jesus searches for the beneficiary of his power. With dramatic detailing, Mark discloses the disconnect between Jesus and his disciples (they are aware of nothing new) and, at the same time, pictures Jesus' eyes circling the crowd, searching for evidence of re-creation.

> "The greatness of Jesus was that he was prepared to pay the price of helping others, and that price was the outgoing of his very life."—Barclay, *The Gospel of Mark*, Daily Study Bible, 132.

For yet the third time in this four-story passage, Jesus' person elicits the emotion of fear in the beneficiary. Mark tells us, in a strange sentence that emphasizes both the permanency of the woman's healing and the permanency of her knowledge of it ("having known what had been done to her," v. 33), that the woman comes forward in fear (*phobos*), falls down, and confesses everything. This is the person Jesus has been searching for and he seals his find with a word of endearment: "Daughter, trusting has saved you; go in peace and be whole" (v. 34). Prior to her confession, she was only healed of chronic affliction. Now, prostrate vulnerably before Jesus, the possibility of a completely ordered, whole existence is hers to claim.

This untouchable embodies the calm of an existence whose chaos has been ruled by the creative power of God. There at Jesus' feet, before the hushed disciples, she worships in the fullness of truth. Using three different descriptors for her grace-filled reality, Jesus emphasizes a completely new creation: *saved, peaceful,* and *whole.*

The Calming of the Future (5:35–43)

With typical Markan restlessness, messengers arrive breathlessly. They speak not to Jesus but directly to Jairus, who has just witnessed Jesus' mastery over a woman's chaotic present. There is no doubt about the reality of their message; indeed, they are blunt about it: "Your daughter has died; let Jesus go" (v. 35). Like primordial waves surging from the watery deep, these words flood Jairus' future. As any parent who has suffered such a loss will testify, Jairus is drowning.

Jesus overhears these harbingers of chaos and preempts Jairus' despair: "Do not fear; only trust" (v. 36). To the storm-tossed disciples, Jesus declared, "You are still not trusting." To the outcast woman, Jesus affirmed, "Trusting has saved you." And to Jairus, as the sun sets on his dark night of the soul, Jesus commands, "Trust only." For Mark, trust is the opposite—and antidote—to fear. Human trust and divine re-creation form an organic whole. Each always includes the other.

Want to Know More?

About sleep? See Leland Ryken, James C. Wilhoit, and Tremper Longman III, eds., *Dictionary of Biblical Imagery* (Downers Grove, Ill.: InterVarsity Press, 1998), 799–800.

About Jesus and power? See Daniel L. Migliore, *The Power of God* (Philadelphia: Westminster Press, 1983), 53–59.

About untouchables? See George Arthur Buttrick, ed. *The Interpreter's Dictionary of the Bible,* vol. A–D (Nashville: Abingdon Press, 1962), 641–48.

As this story climaxes, we see that Mark has curiously bracketed the entire pericope with sleeping. Jesus slept soundly inside the jaws of death at the outset of this passage; here at the end, Jairus' daughter sleeps soundly inside the jaws of death. At every point in this narrative, Jesus defies the power of death to rule the future of humanity. How he does it here is, once again, scandalous. Jesus turns to the professional mourners, who were employed upon declaration of the girl's death, and he tells them they are premature in their duty: "The child is alive and sleeping."

Here we ask *whether* the child actually had died and *when* she had been raised from the dead, if indeed she had been raised. The common interpretation is that Jesus is using a euphemism for death to make a point and to prepare them for the resurrection that is soon to come, and that the girl is really dead. Williamson (109) offers a tempting variation on this reading: "The text intends to affirm that in the presence of Jesus and under his authority death itself, real death, is but a sleep."

An alternate interpretation that maintains the flow of this passage is that Jesus is telling the truth in verse 39 (the girl is literally sleeping) *and* that the messengers are telling the truth in verse 35 (the girl had died), and that somewhere between verses 35 and 39, the girl's life was mysteriously restored—and Jairus' future re-created. In a tantalizing way, Mark leaves us wondering whether this is the purpose and power of Jesus' intrusive command to Jairus in verse 36: "Trust *now*. Jairus, return your future *now* to the hands of the one who originally forged creation out of chaos. Your daughter is a formless void and darkness covers her face, but a wind from God can sweep over her face. Trust, Jairus, and raise your child *now*."

They—and we—laugh long and hard at Jesus because we are bewildered by him. So he casts us from the sanctuary, holds her hand, speaks the truth of her father's trust, nudges the girl awake, and returns the household to an ordinary Palestinian day.

Now we are certain of Jesus' power to reorder our existence. No longer need we imagine ourselves imprisoned by our past or as victims of a past conveniently foisted upon us. No longer need we be defined by the circumstances and pressures of our present. No longer need we fear the permanent loss of our future. Wherever the watery abyss surges over the gunwale of the church, we are confident our cry will be heard. Now we are sure that Jesus' Lordship "knows no bounds" (Williamson, 108).

"Peace! Be still!"

Questions for Reflection

1. The wind and sea story is powerful. Check these references: Genesis 1:2; Exodus 14:21; Psalm 147:18; and Proverbs 30:4.

What answer do these references offer to the disciples' question in Mark 4:41? Who then is Jesus?

2. The story of Mark 5:1–20 is interesting, particularly verse 3: "He lived among the tombs; and no one could restrain him anymore." Some suggest this verse foreshadows Mark 16:1–8. What are some similarities between these two passages?

3. The writer of this unit makes reference to the power of Jesus and "the scandal of its availability." What do you think that phrase means? What are the implications of this available power of Jesus?

4. What are the examples of fear and trusting that are found in the stories of this unit? What things are frightening today? In what things do people place trust? What word of encouragement do these stories offer to the fearful?

The Mystery Scandalizes

We left Jesus at the bedside of Jairus' little girl, whom Jesus had just awakened from death. He was ordering Jairus and his disciples to feed the child, as if there were no greater need on earth in that moment than for the risen child to break fast.

One hundred and fifteen verses later, we find ourselves at the northern tip of the Sea of Galilee in the climax of Jesus' ministry. His work among us is nearly complete. In a moment, Jesus will retreat with his disciples to Caesarea Philippi for a crucial test of their discipleship. Then he and they will plunge toward Jerusalem for their final moments together.

This passage has long been recognized as the pivot or fulcrum of Mark's entire narrative, standing almost dead-center and signaling a shift in Jesus' ministry "from public demonstrations of authority . . . to instruction of the disciples" (Williamson, 4). This passage introduces a whole section of Mark's narrative (8:22–10:52) that Williamson titles, "Discipleship: The Way of Jesus." Before we examine this narrative crux in detail, let us note the direction Jesus' ministry has taken since the awakening of Jairus' daughter.

Jesus' ministry around the Sea of Galilee concludes with the following series of events and encounters:

- Jesus suffers rejection by his hometown (6:1–6).
- Jesus sends the Twelve out empty-handed, to proclaim and exorcise (6:7–13).
- Herod beheads John the Baptist, leaving Jesus with sole authority (6:14–29).

- Jesus corrects the disciples' near-sightedness and feeds five thousand (6:30–44).
- Jesus walks on water and calms a second storm on the Sea of Galilee, but the disciples grow in their confusion and hard-heartedness (6:45–52).
- Jesus returns to the neighborhood of the Gerasene and heals hundreds (6:53–56).
- Jesus defends his Jewishness against an assault by the Pharisees and redefines Jewish faith, but the disciples fail to see (7:1–23).
- Jesus exorcizes a Gentile woman's daughter, admiring her persistence (7:24–30).
- Jesus heals a deaf and mute Gentile man (7:31–37).
- Jesus looks with compassion on four thousand hungry followers and feeds them, but is later bewildered by the disciples' intensifying failure to understand (8:1–21).

Thus we come to the village of Bethsaida on the northern shore of the Sea of Galilee with a paradoxical picture of Jesus and his disciples: the more Jesus ministers, the *less* the disciples grasp his ministry. And the less the disciples grasp his ministry, the more frustrated Jesus becomes, until he pours forth a startling litany: "Do you still not perceive or understand? Are your hearts hardened? Do you have eyes, and fail to see? Do you have ears, and fail to hear? Do you not remember?" (8:14–21).

The more Jesus needs community, the more Jesus finds himself isolated, alone, and misunderstood. Having earlier lost the eyes and ears of his nuclear family, Jesus took confidence that he retained "family" in those who hungered for God's will (3:31–35). But as the religious authorities lower the noose round his neck, Jesus recognizes that even the disciples' eyes and ears are closing. This is how Mark prepares us for the moment of truth in Jesus' ministry with his disciples.

"Whose image is on the coin?"

How Shall We See? (8:22–26)

What does it mean to be called and sent by Jesus Christ, the Son of God?

58

What does it mean to be his disciple? This question is the reason Mark writes his Gospel for the church. The answer is neither quick nor easy.

As the story unfolds toward this climax, Mark skillfully draws us into the disciples' escalating confusion over Jesus. He makes it easy for us as readers to criticize their hardheartedness. But before we know it, we are faced with the same paradox that bewildered them: *Jesus can be known only as he is followed.* This is why Jesus cannot be known by the crowds in the Gospels. This is why Jesus is misunderstood by his own disciples. And this is why Jesus is misapprehended by the church today. Jesus will be known only as he is followed. The act of following contains within itself the education.

Any who demand to understand Jesus *before* they will follow him cripple themselves with an impossible condition. This is the behavior of the crowds and, increasingly, of the disciples. They wish the blessing of Jesus' company apart from the cost of his discipleship. They want to look but not truly to see. They want to listen but not truly to hear. Jesus recognizes this fatal dynamic and makes this the central teaching moment in his ministry: "To know me, you must follow me."

Enter the blind man from Bethsaida, an account that Mark crafts as a lesson on discipleship. This story has intrigued interpreters because it is the only time Jesus applies his healing energy to the same individual twice and it is the only time Jesus actually inquires about the status of the healing he has set in motion. Some have taken this "healing in two parts" to be a comforting reminder that even Jesus Christ struggled against the powers of darkness; that success did not always come easily for Jesus Christ; that there were times when even the Son of God was forced to apply himself doubly.

> "The positioning of this story in the Gospel suggests that what the reader has been led to see of Jesus up to this point, namely his wonder-working power, his authority even to forgive sins, and his enormous popularity with the crowds, represents only a partial vision of who he is."—Williamson, *Mark,* Interpretation, 148.

Such a reading not only demeans Mark's narrative skill, it undermines Mark's purpose. Before we are whisked off by Jesus to Caesarea Philippi for the mother of all retreats on Christian discipleship, Mark uses this encounter with a blind man to characterize Christian discipleship as the gift of sight which we must actively receive.

Notice Mark's emphasis on seeing and looking in this story. Touching the blind man's eyes for the first time, Jesus asks, "Are you seeing anything?" (v. 23). The narrator tells us that the blind man looks up and responds, "I see people that I perceive as trees walking" (v. 24). Jesus touches his eyes a second time. Then in an odd sentence (v. 25) we are told that the man's eyes (plural verb) "looked through" (a word that could mean "looked or focused intently"), that "he" restores (singular verb), and that as a result he is now looking on all things clearly. The sentence could be translated: "Jesus placed hands upon his eyes and they looked intently and he restored and he was looking on all things clearly." What is Mark trying to show us?

Mark carefully prefaces his section on discipleship with this profound image of Jesus "re-forming" a man's capacity to see. Jesus stages this gift of sight in two movements to emphasize that there is more to Christian discipleship than the first glance. Mark might have employed the adage "There's more than meets the eye" to clarify that being a disciple is far more than it appears to be at first. A commitment based only on first sight will not stand the test of discipleship. Mark could be warning the church that it is better to remain blind than to be satisfied with the truth of Jesus half-seen.

Mark wants the church to understand that Christian discipleship is possible because of the miraculous grace of God, but Christian discipleship is not a superficial, passive lifestyle. In Mark's telling, the blind man's sight is not truly restored until he himself looks intently. Like the blind man from Bethsaida, a disciple actively participates with Jesus in the miracle of seeing. A disciple does not merely look up (*ana-blepo*, v. 24) and accept a blurry first glance at the truth, a disciple strives with the Lord's help to look through (*dia-blepo*, v. 25) until he or she is looking on (*em-blepo*, v. 25) all things clearly. Disciples have been given eyes to see what is true and disciples must use their eyes to focus on what is true. How else can we be useful to Jesus Christ in his moment of need?

> "Integrity in confessing the name of Jesus Christ is measured by consistency in following him on his way."—Williamson, *Mark, Interpretation*, 151.

How Shall We Abide by What We See? (8:27–9:1)

Having clarified that Christian disciples should focus their sight(s), Jesus removes his disciples to the northern reaches of Palestine for an engagement in "the heart of the matter" (Williamson, 150). Thus we come to one of the most widely recognizable passages in the Synoptic Gospels—and one of the most challenging to interpret faithfully. Once again, the peril of this passage for the church is its familiarity.

This passage forms a bridge between Jesus' public ministry in Galilee and his private journey to Jerusalem, which will culminate in his arrest and crucifixion. Everything turns with this encounter between Jesus and his chosen Twelve. No longer will the disciples stand alongside Jesus' ministry, or even co-minister with him; from now on, they themselves *become* Jesus' ministry. No longer will Jesus pepper his ministry with mighty acts of charity or healing for the masses, now Jesus peppers us with *demands*.

The structure of this important passage is the key to its interpretation. In Bethsaida, Jesus asked the blind man about his vision, "Are you seeing?" Here on the way to Caesarea Philippi, Jesus will ask about the crowd's vision, "How are they seeing?" Lastly, Jesus will inquire into our vision, "What are you seeing?" Jesus desires disciples whose sight pierces the darkness.

There is an interesting play between the disciples and the crowd. Jesus and his disciples are on their way to the villages of Caesarea Philippi, a heavily Romanized Canaanite village, twenty miles north of the Sea of Galilee. This would be a two- or three-day journey and various travelers would join and leave the band of disciples along the way. Note that in verses 27–33 Jesus is conversing with his disciples and that in verses 34–38 Jesus enlarges the conversation to include the crowd. We might call the substance of his conversation with the disciples "the nature of the *Christ* (Messiah)," while the substance of his conversation with the crowd we might call "the nature of the *Christian*."

Is this not ironic? Jesus clarifies the Christ to Christians, then turns and clarifies the Christian to non-Christians. Moreover, his conversation with the Christians is full of rebuking, whereas his conversation with the non-Christians is full of imperatives. Aren't things reversed? Shouldn't the Christians need enlightenment about being Christian and non-Christians need enlightenment about Christ?

Jesus' conversation with the disciples collapses. At this critical point in the ministry of Jesus, this important private briefing with the disciples unravels in rebuke and confusion. At verse 34, on the heels of his rebuke of Peter, Jesus throws back his head in frustration, turns, and conveys the Christian's vocation to the crowd (within earshot of the disciples). It's a pitiful scene. What should have by now been clear to the disciples gets spent on the crowds. How does it go awry? And why does this same word about discipleship continue to elude and perturb the church to this day?

Jesus has arranged this final retreat to consolidate the disciples' identity before they march to Jerusalem. He wants to prepare them for the long haul. He has planned a simple, two-part agenda: (1) to clarify and consolidate the identity of the Christ; and (2) to clarify and consolidate the identity of the Christian. He would tell the disciples that the vocation of the Christian rightly derives from the vocation of the Christ. He knew it would be rough. But he did not know it would go bust.

He starts strategically by setting the backdrop against which he will unfurl the truth: "How are folk seeing me?" The disciples respond appropriately (and revealingly for the first-century popular impression of Jesus), "John the Baptist resurrected . . . Elijah forerunning the Christ . . . a classic prophet restoring the long-gone Golden Era of the Hebrew prophets."

Then Jesus turns and pops the question to them, "How do you see me?" Actually, the Greek is emphatic, employing an unnecessary extra pronoun for the addressee, "But you, who are *you* declaring me to be?"

Peter, self-appointed press secretary for the Twelve, cocks his shoulders and pronounces, "You are the Christ." Which, astonishingly, draws the rebuke of Jesus: "Don't tell a soul! Keep this to yourselves!"

The Heart of the Matter—Being the Christ (8:31–33)

These verses contain the core truth of Christianity, the vocation of the Christ and the derivative vocation of the Christian. Jesus plants his feet and takes a long, deep breath. He is about to test the fabric of our faith, as never before. Mark even has the narrator alert us: "And with outspokenness, [Jesus] was declaring the word" (v. 31). Jesus is aware of the risk. And he begins.

He begins to teach about the Christ by first subordinating the title Christ (Messiah) to the title Son of Man (Humanity) (v. 31). He is saying, "The Son of Humanity establishes the vocation of the Christ. Not you, Peter. Not you, disciples. And certainly not the crowds." Then Jesus explains why. The Son of Humanity defines the Messiah because the Son of Hu-

Want to Know More?

About the biblical image of seeing? See Leland Ryken, James C. Wilhoit, and Tremper Longman III, eds., *Dictionary of Biblical Imagery* (Downers Grove, Ill.: InterVarsity Press, 1998), 255–56.

About the "messianic secret"? See Eduard Schweizer, *The Good News according to Mark* (Atlanta: John Knox Press, 1970), 54–56.

manity reveals that the other side of God's power is *authority in the form of weakness.*

Until now the Christ has disclosed God's reign in the more visible—and more popular—form of strength and triumph. Following this conversation, the Christ discloses God's reign in the less visible—and much less popular—form of weakness and defeat. In the end, it will be the *whole* ministry of the Christ that testifies to God's reign on earth: in might and in weakness, in triumph and in defeat, visible and invisible.

Jesus is declaring that which sets the Christian faith apart from all other monotheistic religions: that God's will is for the Christ—the almighty Savior of the world—to redeem all things via suffering, rejection, murder, and resurrection. "The death of Jesus on the cross is the *center* of all Christian theology," says Jürgen Moltmann, one of today's leading theologians. "The meaning is that *this* is God, and God is like *this*. God is not greater than [Jesus] is in this humiliation. God is not more glorious than [Jesus] is in this self-surrender. God is not more powerful than [Jesus] is in this helplessness. God is not more divine than [Jesus] is in this humanity"(Moltmann, 204–5). Moltmann helps us walk in the disciples' shoes as the radical news of God in Christ slams into their lives that afternoon on the road to Caesarea Philippi.

This passage has huge significance for the plot of the Gospel story, but it also has huge significance for Christian theology. Heretofore the notion of "the crucified God" was absent from all world religion.

> "The question becomes, 'Knowing now where the winding path will lead, will we follow him?'"—Alyce M. McKenzie, *Matthew*, Interpretation Bible Studies (Louisville, Ky.: Geneva Press, 1998), 64.

The disciples are completely unprepared for it. They have nothing to draw upon to process the concept of a suffering, messianic Savior. They are dumbstruck. And angry.

So Peter pulls Jesus aside and chastises him for the non-sense of his disclosure (v. 32). Then Jesus—still in Peter's private company—turns his body toward the disciples (and his back toward Peter) and begins to rebuke Peter publicly to the other eleven (not to mention the crowd). Note how thoroughly Jesus communicates (v. 33). He uses body language to emphasize the point: "Peter, you are absolutely opposed to me!"

At this critical juncture in the narrative we must not lessen Jesus' rebuke, for on Jesus' rebuke hangs the integrity of the Christian faith. Our gut instinct is to suggest that Jesus is exaggerating, that he cannot possibly mean that Peter is Satan (or even that Peter is acting like Satan). Yet Mark puts it very clearly in the Greek: "Peter, you are Satan because your mind is tuned for the will of human beings, not for the will of God."

Jesus rebukes Peter because Peter behaves no differently than the scribes in unit 2 who came to Jesus declaring, "You have Beelzebul, and by the ruler of the demons you cast out demons! . . . You have an unclean spirit!" (Mark 3:22, 30). In resisting Jesus' self-disclosure as one in whose weakness God will reign in power, the disciples show themselves to be as blind to Jesus as the Jerusalem scribes. In effect, the disciples are blaspheming against the Holy Spirit—committing the dreaded "unforgivable sin"—by contradicting the person and mission of Jesus.

As with the scribes in chapter 2, this is not a matter of misunderstanding the gospel, this is an absolute inversion of the good news of God's reign in Jesus Christ into the evil news of populist, messianic politics. The disciples want Jesus to fulfill the role of the Messiah as the crowd desires rather than reveal the other side of God's startlingly comprehensive power. By refusing to imagine Jesus as the Messiah who will suffer, the disciples set themselves against Jesus and lock themselves in a state of moral blindness. Jesus has no choice but to turn his back in opposition. Make no mistake about it, on Jesus' rebuke hangs the integrity of the Christian faith.

The Heart of the Matter—Being a Christian (8:34–9:1)

As Jesus rebukes the disciples, he turns to include the crowd in his revelation about being the Christian. We have already noted the irony of this—for the Christians, Jesus clarifies the Christ; but for the non-Christians, Jesus clarifies the Christian—and have suggested that Jesus' agenda collapses with the disciples' impenetrableness. In frustration, Jesus openly shares the conversation with everyone, hoping that some will have eyes to see and ears to hear, "If *anyone* wills to follow after me . . . " (v. 34).

These words of Jesus are often quoted. Perhaps no teaching of his is as sheared into pieces as this one. But we must hold it together. Having just defined the Christ, Jesus now defines the Christian. "A disciple," says Jesus, "is one who denies, takes up, and follows." Williamson (154) cautions against viewing this singular, threefold definition as three distinct definitions, "The threefold condition of discipleship . . . is a single condition, for the first two terms define and specify the third." Self-denial and cross-bearing together constitute obedient discipleship.

Turning to the one congregation of crowd and disciples, Jesus clarifies that a Christian is one who *wills* to be a Christian. Recall the example of the blind man from Bethsaida—a seeing person is one who *wills* to use the gift of sight to see. In other words, being Christian involves willful activity; it is

"Whoever does not take up the cross . . . is not worthy of me."

not a status magically conferred by parents or even baptism. This is why the concept Christian throughout the New Testament is almost exclusively verbal. The noun "Christian" occurs only three times in the New Testament (Acts 11:26; 26:28; and 1 Peter 4:16). Usually the New Testament references the followers of Christ by a description of their active faithfulness.

Jesus then issues three successive commands, which together make up the most concise definition of being Christian in the entire New Testament: deny yourself, take up your cross, and start walking. Let us examine Jesus' personal understanding of discipleship. We shall focus on what Williamson calls the two terms of discipleship, self-denial and cross-bearing.

What does Jesus mean when he commands all would-be followers, "Deny yourself"? The word behind "deny" is a Greek word that Mark uses only here and in 14:30 to describe Peter's crushing denial of Jesus Christ ("Truly I tell you, this day, this very night, before the cock crows twice, you will *deny* me three times"; Mark 14:30, NRSV, emphasis added). The Greek word for "deny" can be translated "disown" or "renounce claim to," connoting an intentional act of disassociation from a particular relationship: "have nothing more to do with." Mark's reserved use of this word is provocative. Could he be suggesting that being a Christian involves denying self, yet even the most forthright of Christians (Peter) could still deny Jesus Christ? Could Mark be suggesting that Christian willfulness remain humble, aware that even the most intimately related and rightly confessing Christian is subject to betrayal?

As we struggle with the notion of self-denial, we must confess that this imperative has been mishandled in three disastrous ways. First, some have used Jesus' definition of Christian for a sociological purpose, to keep folk in their place. For example, Christian slaves, battered housewives, and persons battling depression have, at times, been exhorted to accept their reality, to deny themselves, and to remain as they are. Second, some have used Jesus' definition of Christian for a materialistic purpose, to get folk to share their stuff. For example, preachers have found self-denial especially convenient during the annual stewardship campaign. Third, some have used Jesus' definition of Christian for a psychological purpose, to coax folk to disown themselves. For example, a pastoral counselor who is personally opposed to women in ministry might counsel a woman to deny herself and her sense of God's call to ordained ministry.

All of these interpretations of self-denial misconstrue the Christian faith! The whole purpose of Jesus Christ is to redeem and to fulfill our humanity. Whatever Jesus means by denying self should not be construed to mean denying our humanity. Quite the contrary, Jesus' command to deny self is Jesus' prescription for *fulfilling* humanity. Furthermore, while Jesus' command to deny self indeed has a severe bearing on our materialism (which degrades humanity), we must not reduce self-denial to an imperative against possessing some thing.

Jesus does not command us to distance ourselves from a relationship with something or someone else, but instead to disassociate ourselves from a *particular relationship we have with ourselves.* Jesus knows that if a disciple wants to be the line-leader the line will never get to Jerusalem. So he states the Christian faith conditionally: "If anyone wills to follow behind me, he or she must remain behind me!" Williamson (154) agrees: "The way of Jesus . . . [is] a denial of the grasping self to liberate the greater one." Said another way, "You must rearrange your relationship with your self so that your self does not lord you, but allows me to be your lord."

> "Disciples are not to guide, protect, or possess Jesus; they are to follow him."—Williamson, *Mark*, Interpretation, 153.

The second term of discipleship is cross bearing. What does Jesus mean when he commands all of us would-be Christians, "Pick up your cross"? Once again, the church has at times fallen prey to temptation and used Jesus' crisp definition to convince us that our cross is whatever ill-fated circumstance or affliction we find ourselves in at the moment. For some, carrying our cross has been equated with bearing a cancer diagnosis bravely or keeping the attitudinal chin up in the face of racism.

As painful as those circumstances are, they miss the impact of the phrase. This is not what the cross meant in the ancient world. And this cannot be what Jesus defines as the core of Christian discipleship. The cross was a particularly ghoulish form of capital punishment reserved for persons who committed a crime against the Roman state. When Jesus defines the Christian disciple as one who picks up his or her cross, he is saying that the disciple must fully bear the cost of doing God's will. The cross for the disciple is identical to the cross for Jesus in that it is the *consequence* (not the condition) of righteousness. The cross is what Jesus Christ was forced to bear for doing God's will.

The rightness or wrongness of the cross, as we are nailed to it, is not the issue. Is it not remarkable that Jesus refuses to quarrel with his prosecutors, despite their glaring injustice? He just quietly takes up the horridly unjust cross that is laid upon him by the Roman-Jewish conspiracy. And he makes it clear that a disciple will do likewise. A disciple will do the will of God at all costs and will accept (pick up) the consequences (cross) that result from his or her right behavior. Jesus is warning the church that doing God's will sometimes has capital consequences, but that disciples will not permit consequences to divert them from the mission of righteousness.

Jesus knows the fearsome force of his teaching about discipleship, and so closes the conversation with a word of encouragement. He declares that discipleship is worth the cost because you will discover life that is more valuable than the cost. In effect, Jesus exhorts the church, "You need not be afraid or ashamed of being my disciple! You need not be afraid or ashamed of being emphatic about the will of God! You need not be afraid or ashamed of be-

> "The call, the warning, and the challenge are significant because they cut clean across the grain of conventional wisdom, popular piety, and natural inclination."— Williamson, *Mark*, Interpretation, 157.

ing capitally punished for doing what is right or good or true. In this you will discover your true humanity. In losing your life, you will gain life that is priceless and permanent. Be not afraid. Get behind me, and follow."

Questions for Reflection

1. The old adage "Seeing is believing" takes on a different meaning after reading this unit. How so?
2. When Jesus asks the disciples, "Who do people say that I am?" they respond by listing several individuals that we (and they) know he could not be. Why would the people think Jesus was John, Elijah, or a prophet? What has become of John or Elijah? Are they alive or dead? Peter's answer is an attempt to correct the people's mistake. Why does Jesus forbid Peter to tell anyone his conclusion?
3. This passage speaks about self-denial and cross bearing. What do these phrases mean for today's faithful?
4. Jesus rebukes Peter, a verb reserved for demonics and the turbulent sea in Mark's Gospel. Did Peter deserve this harsh response by Jesus? Why or why not? What things today deserve to be rebuked?

The Mystery Defies

In this passage Mark creates a dramatic collision between Jesus and the prevailing religious establishment. Mark wants us to appreciate how deadly faith becomes when we institutionalize it. We are in the final week of Jesus' life; Palm Sunday is already behind us, and Good Friday stares at us through the tunnel we know as Holy Week. Over the span of these few verses, Jesus' authority will be challenged by every known office of first-century institutional Judaism: chief priests, scribes, elders, Pharisees, Herodians, and Sadducees. If Temple Judaism can be regarded as a vineyard, then these six authorities are the tenants to whom God has temporarily leased the vineyard. Mark's purpose here is not to degrade Judaism, but to disclose the murderous dynamic of institutionalized religion and to contrast it with the living, Jewish faith of Jesus Christ.

We should recall in this scene that though the Jews had centuries ago returned from exile, rebuilt the Jerusalem Temple, and restored their native roots in Palestinian soil, they lived day-to-day

> "Throughout the history of Israel the leaders of God's people rejected the prophets God sent, preferring to exercise their authority independently of God's authoritative word."—Williamson, *Mark*, Interpretation, 214.

under the occupation of Rome. In Jesus' day, Palestine was an official territory of Rome, ruled by surrogate Roman sovereigns like Herod the Great and Herod Antipas. By and large, the Jews were permitted freedom to practice their faith, though it must have been politically expedient for Jewish leaders to play to Rome's hand.

In this tense mix of religion and politics, Mark is clear that Jesus' life is endangered, not by politicians, but ironically by religious authorities. While it is true that only the Roman state could execute by crucifixion, the Jewish leaders could convince the politicians that such a punishment was in Rome's best interest. We will emerge from this series of confrontations with religious authorities with little doubt that the fate of Jesus Christ has been sealed by a conspiracy between the high Jewish court and Rome.

Before we examine the narrative in detail, let us revisit the immediately preceding moments in Jesus' life. We left him two and a half chapters ago at the end of his retreat on Christian discipleship in Caesarea Philippi (8:22–9:1), at the conclusion of his public ministry in Galilee. In 10:1 we are told that Jesus "left that place" and turned his face to Jerusalem. Since the retreat in Caesarea Philippi, Jesus has experienced the following:

- A dazzling, end-of-retreat transfiguration (9:2–13)
- A healing encounter with a lad convulsed by epilepsy (9:14–29)
- The second forecast of his passion (9:30–32)
- A quarrel among his disciples over their power, prestige, and privilege (9:33–37)
- The disciples' prejudgment of a competing exorcist (9:38–41)
- A warning against leading "little ones" into temptation (9:42–50)
- A pop-quiz by the Pharisees over the legality of divorce (10:1–12)
- Great displeasure over his disciples' restraining order on children (10:13–16)
- An urgent appeal by a man who had everything except eternal life (10:17–31)
- The third and final forecast of his passion (10:32–34)
- A second quarrel among his disciples over power, prestige, and privilege (10:35–45)
- Another healing encounter with a blind man, this time, Bartimaeus (10:46–52)
- A donkey-back parade into Jerusalem (11:1–11)
- A violent encounter in the spiritually fruitless Temple-turned-marketplace (11:12–26)

And so, only midway through this Bible study, Mark lands us in the final 120 hours of Jesus' life. We still have five chapters of Mark's Gospel to go (and half of this study!). The Gospels have been appropriately described as stories that are written backward, or as one scholar remarked, "passion narratives with extended introductions" (cited by Williamson, 4). In other words, we are studying the middle of Jesus' life solely because of the *end* of Jesus' life. Take away the ending, and Jesus' life (including the whole of Christianity) folds itself neatly and anonymously into the archives of history.

Keith Nickle (63) puts it this way:

> Mark's major literary achievement was that of taking the various types of Jesus traditions and welding them to the church's preaching of the crucified and risen Christ. He thereby established controls and set limits for the interpretation of the traditions. He also firmly anchored the church's cross-event proclamation in the history of the earthly Jesus. He was employing the Jesus traditions to provide a broad narrational history which embodied a saving event of eternal dimensions. He described that saving event in the climax to his work, the Passion narrative. We are thereby forced to regard all of the episodes in the public ministry of Jesus as anticipatory prefigurements of the passion. That is, each incident is obscure (and even misleading and deceptive) until it is interpreted from the controlling perspective of the crucifixion and resurrection.

From this point forward, we must not overlook the intractable atmosphere of tension between Jesus and the Jewish leaders. Their relationship had become taut as an overtuned violin string. We can be sure that the whole Jewish culture of Jerusalem was abuzz with gossip, rumors, reports, and sightings. Jesus had become a celebrity in the worse sense, lusted after by the crowds and hunted by the leaders.

In the verses immediately preceding this passage, Jesus crosses the line and violates the religious leaders' consumeristic stake in the Temple marketplace. Mark alerts us that a deathly friction now dominates Jesus' every move: "The chief priests and the scribes . . . kept looking for a way to kill him; for they were afraid of him, because the whole crowd was spellbound by his teaching" (11:18, NRSV). Jesus and his disciples have begun the long spiral into the vortex of death.

What Is the Nature of Authority? (11:27–33)

Jesus leads his band back to Jerusalem, and takes them straight to the Temple, now a disturbed hornet's nest of anti-Jesus sentiment. He is immediately approached by the chief priests, scribes, and presbyters (elders), who come to him with a nagging question about the nature of authority. Their question of authority is really a question of *authorization,* and they are emphatic about it: "By what authority . . . By whose authority do you act like this?" (11:28). This professional

Temple conglomerate is declaring that *they* are the sole authorizers of religious behavior and that *they* have not authorized Jesus' behavior.

This text can be read as Mark's exposition of the perilous nature of faith, when faith becomes a means to an end rather than an end in itself. These divinely appointed stewards of the covenant between God and Israel have perverted their calling to ministry into private enterprise for themselves. Selected to be disciples of the living God—those called to deny their grasping selves and to do what is right at all costs—these leaders have become the antithesis. They have neatly packaged God's relationship with humanity and are selling it at a profit for a corporation on whose board of directors they sit.

Listen to their capitalistic vacillation over Jesus' question: "If we say this, our competitor will gain the upper hand; if we say that, however, our product will not sell" (11:31–32). Their deliberation and discernment are not God-centered, but human-centered. They are not clergy, but populists; not religious, but religionist. They are not managing the institution for the survival of the people's faith; they are managing the people's faith for the survival of the institution!

The tricky part of hearing this Scripture, however, is avoiding the "us-them" game that we readers can so arrogantly play, for Mark would have us know that we are all subject to this temptation of self-serving institutionalization. We are not casual observers or blameless bystanders.

> "This warning originally addressed to arrogant Jewish leaders applies equally to arrogant Christian leaders today."—Williamson, *Mark*, Interpretation, 216.

Jesus will have none of this. Authority for Jesus is theological, relational, and humble. He answers their question like a rabbi, with a counter question (11:30) that is "not an evasion but a serious theological statement" (Williamson, 212). Moreover, Jesus' question is essentially one of John's *relationship* to God, not John's status as the authorizer of an institution. Lastly, though John was publicly regarded as a prophet, his humble existence had not been forgotten.

The board of directors for the Temple is disestablished by Jesus' question. Ironically, their only option is to confess that they have no authority: "We have not known and we continue not to know" (this is the effect of the Greek perfect tense used by them in 11:33). To which Jesus replies, "So be it," and completes the turning of the tables. The Jewish council emerges as authorizer with no authority; Jesus emerges as authority with no interest whatever in authorizing.

The Nature of Authority Is Stewardship (12:1–12)

Having seized the reins from the Temple leadership, Jesus proceeds to speak to them in parables. Let us reimagine this exchange. Jesus returns to the Temple. He is interrogated about his authority by the authorizers. He, in turn, interrogates the authorizers about the nature of authority. The authorizers wilt under the pressure, for they have no real authority. Jesus, in turn, authoritatively withholds a didactic answer to their question and offers in its place a parable. He is ever so subtly in complete command.

This parable bespeaks the audacity of Jesus Christ. Imagine this. Here he stands in the most political place in Jerusalem, face-to-face with the political religionists who hold his fate in their hands, painting a graphic picture of their own abuse of authority. Then Jesus dares to extend the story as a proclamation of the ultimate triumph of God over their abuse of privilege and power. They get a graphic illustration of their murderous stewardship, an assurance that God will transfer the vineyard of Israel's faith to other stewards. Finally, Jesus affirms from their own scripture (Ps. 118) that God will triumph *in spite of* them and *without* them! So much for their authority.

"He will . . . give the vineyard to others."

This parable of the wicked tenants illustrates the Jewish leaders' abuse of authority. Jesus describes their stewardship as violently self-oriented, to the point of murder. They may triumph in the short run, but not in the long.

But this parable also communicates to first-century Christians who are struggling against rising anti-Christian sentiment within Judaism that the stewardship of God's covenant with Israel belongs to them as well. In effect, Mark exhorts the young church to remember the gospel of God's love for all people in Jesus Christ. Williamson (214) describes Mark's rendering as "a moving expression in story form of the gospel of God's beloved Son, which John 3:16 states in a propositional nutshell."

As Williamson (214–15) engages this "Gospel in miniature," he breaks the parable into four parts, suggesting that each part illustrates a particular stage in God's history of salvation. First, as the tenants reject slaves sent by the landowner, so did Israel reject God's prophets. Second, as the tenants refused to respect even the landowner's beloved son, so did these Temple leaders refuse to respect God's Son, Jesus Christ. Third, as the tenants proceeded to murder the landowner's beloved son for self-gain, so did these Jewish authorities of the status quo dispense with God's Son, Jesus Christ. And fourth, as the landowner subsequently transferred stewardship of the vineyard from the original tenants to others, so did God transfer stewardship of the Temple to the church.

Taking the whole story in context, it seeks to communicate the massive abuse of power by those with a vested interest in maintaining the religious status quo. Again, Mark is warning religious leaders of all times and places about the lethal danger of institutionalizing God's living covenant with humanity. Williamson (216) says:

> To all in any position of authority in the church this parable addresses a warning about the dangerous tendency to carve out "our" domain, to forget whose the vineyard is, or, most insidious of all, to refer piously to "the Lord's work" at precisely those times when we are enlisting others to help build our own petty empires.

The Scope of Stewardship Is Limitless (12:13–17)

Mark informs us that as Jesus nears the end of his parable the religious leaders realize that he is telling this parable against them (12:12). They are enraged, but they are also ironically impotent because they must play to the popular vote. The noose is around Jesus' neck, but there is none who can yet tighten it.

So they storm off and send in their stead the Pharisees and Herodians, hoping that they will have the finesse to hang Jesus. The con-

"Whose image is on the coin?"

spiracy against Jesus has spread to every office in the Temple; it has now become an open season on the Son of God. One group after the other from the local ministerial union brings the trap of its trade to snare Jesus. We don't know who the Herodians were, but it seems that their collaboration with the Pharisees was a conspiracy between Temple and throne.

They first try to kill Jesus with kindness by affirming his truthfulness, his impartiality, and his passion for the truth of Torah. Then on the heels of this buttery prelude, they spring the $64,000 question on Jesus: "Is it consistent with Torah to pay taxes to Caesar, or not? Guide us, O you honest, unprejudiced, rabbinic one" (12:14). They have surely cooked this one up in the back halls of the Temple; it exudes their conspiracy to trap Jesus simultaneously on theological and political grounds. If he answers, "Yes, pay Caesar's tax," the Jews will have him for idolatry; if he answers, "No, withhold Caesar's tax," the IRS will have him. His goose is cooked.

Actually, what is cooked is Jesus' temper. Slicing through their doublespeak, Jesus decides to answer this time not didactically nor parabolically, but with an object lesson. He demands a Roman coin and then addresses his fellow Jews, the Pharisees, and Herodians asking: "Whose image and title is this?"

"Piece of cake, Nazarene, it's the Caesar."

The trap has been laid, but it is they (and we) who are snared by it.

In a fascinating irony of history (and theology), this familiar teaching continues to be a trap for us, two thousand years after Jesus set it. Just assemble a group of church folk, introduce this passage, and request their interpretation. Almost everyone will fall headlong into its jaws, with some variation on the theme of two kingdoms: "Certain things in the world belong to the government and certain things in the world belong to God; that's just the way it is." How remarkable it is that church folk today come out no cleaner than first-century Pharisees and Herodians!

The problem is that the Bible—both Old and New Testament—wants nothing to do with a two-kingdom worldview. Such a view not only runs directly against the grain of Jewish faith, but undermines the good news that, in Jesus Christ, God has begun to reign *at home* on earth. Every attempt to divide creation into two kingdoms—one secular and one spiritual—is anti-Semitic, anti-Christian, non-biblical, and ethically disastrous.

What, then, did Jesus mean? The Greek reads, "Give back the things of Caesar to Caesar *kai* the things of God to God." The Greek word *kai* is a conjunction that has different meanings according to the context in which it is used. It is usually translated "and," which, if translated as such here, renders Jesus' teaching in the direction of "two kingdoms": "Give back the things of Caesar to Caesar *and* the things of God to God." This explains why such an interpretation is so prevalent.

But *kai* must not always be translated this way. Another perfectly valid way to translate *kai* is epexegetically. The fancy word "epexegetical" comes from a Greek word that simply means to explain in detail. So if we take this to be Jesus' intent in using the conjunction *kai,* what follows *kai* will be the *detailed explanation* of that which precedes *kai.* "Give back the things of God to God" becomes Jesus' *detailed explanation* of "Give back the things of Caesar to Caesar." One translation could be: "Give back the things of Caesar to Caesar, *that is,* the things of God to God!" Or even better, "Give back the things of Caesar to Caesar; *what I mean is,* the things of God to God!"

This is no small matter, for with this tiny teaching Jesus plays his theological trump card and recasts *every* human action as theologically significant. He is declaring to those who have found it convenient to compartmentalize life into two kingdoms that *all* human behavior is theological—that *every* action has to do with God, even the most mundane, such as filing Form 1040 with the IRS. To behave any other way, as religious leaders, is to behave with diminished authority, for real authority is the authority of *stewardship.* The more all-embracing the stewardship, the greater the authority.

> "One's ultimate loyalty, one's personhood, belongs to God alone. In an ultimate sense, so does all of creation."—Williamson, *Mark,* Interpretation, 219.

To paraphrase Jesus on this thorny teaching, "The things of Caesar are but a tiny, tiny subset of the things of God, for God owns everything! Those who understand this and embody this in their words and actions are those with authentic authority."

Those Whose God Is Dead Cannot Be Stewards (12:18–27)

Only one school within first-century Judaism remains to try Jesus' wisdom, the Sadducees. Well, here he stands, and here they come. We don't know much about this group which existed for less than two hundred years, but we know enough. The Sadducees were a short-lived, aristocratic party who did not believe in the resurrection or in angels or spirits of any kind. They adhered only to the first part of the Hebrew Scriptures, the *Torah* (the Hebrew designation of the first five books of the Old Testament); they rejected the authority of the second part of the Hebrew Bible, the Prophets (in Hebrew, *Neviim*), and the third part, the Writings (in Hebrew, *Kethuvim*). So the Sadducees abided by only one-third of the Hebrew Scriptures! In addition, they also rejected the scribal and Pharisaic interpretive traditions. They were a persnickety lot. They were also affluent, literalistic, cynical, and secularist—personality attributes that most often transmute into self-sufficiency, narrow-mindedness, skepticism, and worldliness.

They approach Jesus with a "Torah-teaser" on levirate marriage. The Sadducees' aim in this encounter is hard to grasp. Perhaps it is an attempt to one-up Jesus on a basic Bible exam. Their question is laughable, contorted, and innocuous. Would Jesus ensnare himself by addressing such a wildly pitched scenario (is this a moment of Markan comic relief)? The practice of levirate marriage can be found in Deuteronomy 25:5–10; it was an attempt to protect a deceased man's stake in his family long after his death.

Here's the scene, in all its hilarity. The Sadducees stroll up to Jesus, surround him, toss their lacy, purple togas over their shoulders, clear their throats, reach deep into their Torah for the case law on levirate marriage, stretch the case into absurdity, and drop it in Jesus' lap, in hopes they will emerge superior to this young whippersnapper of a rabbi. What makes this scenario even more ludicrous is that the Sadducees conclude their trickery with a sarcastic stab at the resurrection (12:23), which everybody knows they sneer at. Their smugness is almost audible in the text. They stroke one another in adulation.

Jesus is not amused. This entire series of encounters has been about religious authority, something near and dear to Jesus' heart. He regards the offices of Judaism very highly, even if he encounters few role models. These are men called and gifted by the Lord of Israel to be stewards of Israel's life with God. Jesus does not take kindly to this litany of ridicule within the house of prayer. He nears the end of his rope.

He begins and ends with the charge that the Sadducees have gone astray (12:24)—even "plentifully astray" (12:27). They have wandered from and abandoned what is true and right for Israel. Jesus' opening volley is the serious charge of stewardship forsaken. He has begun, in effect, to inform the Sadducees that they are *no longer* authorities for Israel. How can they possibly retain authority (the original subject of this passage), if they are currently ignorant of both the

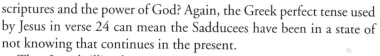

scriptures and the power of God? Again, the Greek perfect tense used by Jesus in verse 24 can mean the Sadducees have been in a state of not knowing that continues in the present.

Then Jesus brilliantly segues (12:25) to a theological stance the Sadducees have just parodied, the resurrection. He declares, "*When* the seven brothers and their wife *rise from the dead*," emphasizing the reality of the resurrection. Then, to the Sadducees' embarrassment, Jesus pronounces their other two theological errors, "they neither marry nor are given in marriage, but are like angels in heaven." He probably strategically raises his voice, so that the phrases *"Rise from the dead"* . . . *neither marry . . . like angels"* echo through the Temple corridors. The Sadducean countenance has never been so crimson.

> "Belief in the resurrection of decayed bodies seemed like a foolish superstition to many then as now. The New Testament writers make it clear, however, that when they speak of resurrection they are not thinking of the restoration of physical bodies to their predeath state."—Hare, *Mark, Westminster Bible Companion*, 157.

But Jesus is not finished. He returns to the doctrine of the resurrection. For Jesus and his deep first-century Jewish faith, "the dead being raised" is of central importance. So Jesus dives to the heart of the Sadducees' Bible, the Torah—the "burning bush" story in Exodus 3—wherein the Holy One of Israel intimately reveals the proper name for God, "YHWH," and with the name, God's nature and character and purpose and power. There is no story in the Hebrew Scripture more potent with divine self-disclosure than this one.

Jesus' use of the scripture is very shrewd. "When God speaks to Moses (who lived generations after Abraham, Isaac, and Jacob had died), how can God use the *present* tense, 'I *am being* their God,' if Abraham, Isaac, and Jacob are not alive and well? In other words, Messrs. Sadducees, God uses the *present* tense to Moses because they *have been raised from the dead* and are, this very moment, *alive and well!* You have not gone merely astray, my friends, you have gone *greatly* astray" (12:27).

Jesus lacerates the Sadducean authority. He has pronounced that these lords of Israel's faith not only stand in a perpetual state of ignorance over the scriptures and the mighty acts of God, but that their theology is bankrupt. In effect, Jesus is declaring that God is dead for the Sadducees and that they are perfectly unfit to be the stewards of Israel's faith. Let it be known that those for whom God is dead lack all authority.

Behold, the Authority of Stewardship! (12:28–34)

Mark concludes with a lone scribe overhearing Jesus' conversation with the Sadducees. The scribe so appreciates the integrity of Jesus' response that he queries the rabbi about the central tenet of Jewish faith: "Which commandment is first of all?" (v. 28).

We must never accuse Mark of condemning Judaism. He most certainly is not. And we most certainly must not. In its chastisement of the various offices within first-century Temple Judaism, the New Testament skirts along the edge of anti-Semitism. Because of this, many in the church have fallen off this edge and have seen in the New Testament a wholesale condemnation of Jewish faith. Nothing has been (and could be) more disastrous for Christianity than this. Suffice it to say, the New Testament provides glimpses that both confirm Christianity's enthusiastic embrace of the core tenets of Jewish faith and admonish Christianity's ongoing observance of the tenets of Judaism.

Jesus responds to the genuinely curious scribe with what is known as the Shema (named such because the first Hebrew word in the Mosaic commandment in Deuteronomy 6:4 is *shema,* meaning "hear," or better, "obey"). This Jewish confession is still repeated by observant Jews at the close of the day. To this funda-mental of Israel's commandments Jesus fuses a second commandment, a much lesser commandment also within the Torah, Leviticus 19:18, "You shall love your neighbor as yourself" (NRSV). Here Jesus raises our mutual humanity to the same holy orbit as God's Lordship, a concept deeply at the heart of Judaism but neglected by these particularly sloppy stewards of Israel.

Want to Know More?

About the different types of Jewish religious leaders? See Alyce M. McKenzie, *Matthew,* Interpretation Bible Studies (Louisville, Ky.: Geneva Press, 1998), 3.

About Jewish understandings of death and resurrection in the time of Jesus? See Werner H. Schmidt, *The Faith of the Old Testament: A History* (Philadelphia: Westminster Press, 1983), 266–77.

About the practice of crucifixion? See William Barclay, *The Gospel of Luke,* Daily Study Bible, rev. ed. (Philadelphia: Westminster Press, 1975), 282–86.

"Only as we see in the gift of his life 'a ransom for many' can we bear to hear his word about the great commandment. Yet the cross, far from obliterating the command, reinforces it as love calls forth love. How shall we respond to one who gives his life for us?"— Williamson, *Mark,* Interpretation, 230.

The scribe erupts in ecstasy over Jesus' wisdom and begins gushing with two further scriptural affirmations—"there is no other" (Isa. 45:5; Dan. 3:29; Joel 2:27) and "this is much more important than all whole burnt offerings and sacrifices" (Hos. 6:6; Micah 6:6–8). Notice that these two scriptural affirmations include the prophetic literature, that part of the Hebrew Scriptures not considered authoritative by the Sadducees. Like a tuning fork, Jesus resonates with the scribe's wisdom and pays him the highest compliment, "God is nearly reigning in your life" (Mark 12:34).

Mark concludes with this sublime example of spiritual authority. This eager, anonymous scribe becomes "the only teacher of the Law to be mentioned affirmatively in Mark" (Williamson, 225). Innocently overhearing the debate while passing, he humbly and exuberantly shows himself to be the living answer to the Jewish council's original concern in 11:28, "What is the nature of authority?"

"The nature of authority is *stewardship*," says Jesus, "stewardship of the love of God and humanity. There is no higher authority for religious leaders."

? Questions for Reflection

1. This unit treats the tension between Jesus and the religious establishment of his day. What would the tensions be today if Jesus were to come to church?

2. How does one gain authority? What are the sources of authority today? How do people use religion as an authority? Where does Jesus claim his authority lies?

3. Jesus entertains a discussion about the resurrection to say that it will be like an angelic existence. What do you think that means? What images do you use when you speak about the resurrection?

4. This passage ends with the affirmation, "You are not far from the kingdom of God" (12:34, NRSV), words many of us would long to hear. What is it that the scribe has done which makes him not far from the kingdom? Was the scribe affirmed because he agreed with Jesus' answers, or was the scribe affirmed because he (the scribe) had correctly made sacrifice subservient to love? Why do you think so?

The Mystery Urges

Here in the thick of Jesus' final week on earth, we come to a beguiling passage, perhaps more so than anything else in the entire New Testament. This passage is beguiling because the final week in the life of Jesus Christ is beguiling. Mark is unable to tell the story of this week without signaling its atrocity. This chapter is Mark's signal flare. Here he attempts to jolt the church awake for the rest of human history as we know it.

In order to jar us, Jesus assumes a whole new way of speaking, with peculiar vocabulary, tone, and frame of reference. We are meant to be shocked out of all lethargy and slumber. The time is urgent. Jesus Christ, the Son of God, is hours from betrayal. We have followed him all the way to this point. He has never needed us more awake, alert, and watching than he needs us now. Everything is at stake.

On the one hand, the church's handling of this extraordinary passage has produced a comedy of errors. On the other hand, even in its weirdest interpretive moments, the church has illustrated that the appropriate posture of Christian life is one of peaceful urgency. Such is the nature of this literature. As we rejuvenate our stewardship of this strange and wonderful text, let us

"From the fig tree learn its lesson."

81

abandon any certitudes about the world's end. But let us also preserve a fervor that will keep us alert.

Let us abandon judgment too. Perhaps no New Testament passage has given birth to more judgment between Christians than Mark 13 (not to mention judgment between denominations!). Of course it is *not* faithful for Christian sisters and brothers to passionately promote the precise day, hour, and minute of Jesus' return, but it *is* faithful for sisters and brothers to be *passionate*. On the other hand, it is *not* faithful for Christian sisters and brothers to live boring and slothful lives, but it *is* faithful for sisters and brothers to refrain from obsessive details about the end of time. Williamson (235–36) captures well the riptide that this chapter creates within the church:

> The thirteenth chapter of Mark is a happy hunting ground for persons fascinated by the end of the world. It figures prominently in books by doomsayers and in sermons by evangelists more interested in the next world than in this one. On the other hand, this chapter is largely ignored by pragmatists, activists, believers in progress, and all who dismiss preoccupation with the end of the world as a juvenile state of human development or an aberration of unbalanced minds.

This passage is so unusual that it has been given a variety of names. Mark 13 has been called the Synoptic Apocalypse or the Little Apocalypse. The word "apocalypse" is a transliteration of the Greek word which means "uncovering" or "revelation." "Little" simply indicates that it is a miniature revelation of the end of time compared to John's major Apocalypse, the book of the New Testament we know more familiarly as "The Revelation to John." Chapter 13 has also been called Jesus' Eschatological Discourse. "Eschatology" comes from the Greek word that means last and defines that area of theology that studies the history of thought about the end of the known world.

The designation Eschatological Discourse leads us to emphasize the *context* and *structure* of chapter 13 as keys to the chapter's meaning and purpose. We have already noted that Mark locates chapter 13 in the thick of suspense, just "two days before the Passover and the festival of Unleavened Bread" (14:1). In a matter of hours, Jesus and the disciples will be separated until the end of time. Williamson (236–38) notes that this passage forms Jesus' "longest unbroken speech in Mark" and, as such, functions as Jesus' farewell discourse, his last word to the disciples. Indeed, this entire speech poignantly takes place in the Mount of Olives, less than five hundred yards from the Temple, immediately after the disciples and their master have exited the Temple for the last time. Jesus and the Twelve move from the Temple to the Mount of Olives for one last lecture on the end of time.

The overall structure of this passage is most important to grasp. More often than not, readers dive headlong into this thicket and are lost forever. Instead, let us stand awhile at the edge before diving into the thorny particulars. If we are patient, we will see that the structure of this chapter is a simple question by the disciples (13:4) and a long-winded answer by Jesus (13:5–37). A more subtle element of its structure is the fivefold recurrence of the verb "see" by Jesus, occurring at the beginning of the conversation in question form (13:2) and then four more times in command form, "Be able to see!" (13:5, 9, 23, 33).

The verb "see" recalls Mark's model figure for discipleship in Mark 8:22–9:1, the blind man from Bethsaida (see unit 5). We remember that a disciple of Jesus Christ does not merely "look up" and accept a blurry, first glance at the truth. A disciple strives within the Lord's hands to "look through" until he or she is "look-ing on" (focusing on) all things clearly. As the end nears, Jesus Christ cries out for followers who passionately exercise their gift of sight.

> "To the same disciples to whom he had said 'Follow!' Jesus will now add the command, 'Watch!' "—Williamson, *Mark*, Interpretation, 237.

Last, and perhaps most important, let us read this text more for its *emotional* charge than for its historical particulars about the end of time. Jesus is much more interested in disciples whose lives confidently testify to God's sovereign reign in the world than he is in disciples who fancy themselves adept with proof-texting about who, what, when, where, why, and how. Jesus is rendering an *artistic image* of disciple-ship; he is not crunching an analytical flowchart to the last day.

This is why Jesus fills the lecture with emotionally charged verbs like "see" (13:2, 5, 9, 23, 33), "alarm" (13:7), "worry-ahead-of-time" (13:11), "endure" (13:13), "keep alert" (13:33), and "keep watch" (13:34, 35, 37). His primary aim in this last circle with his beloved is not the communication of data or knowledge or details, but the in-spiration that leads to calm, patient, courageous endurance. Mark 13 is a corrective word of hope to the church in a difficult moment. In short, it is Jesus' impressionistic masterpiece of the character of Chris-tian discipleship. We are to stand before it as long as it takes to rub off on our theological imagination.

On the surface, Jesus' farewell speech springs from a brief exchange with his disciples as they are departing the Temple; they pose a sim-ple question and Jesus responds at length:

Verses 1–2   Initial Exchange
Verses 3–4   Disciples' Question: "When? What signs?"
Verses 5–37 Jesus' Answer: "Stay awake! Only the Father knows."

Below the surface, the substance of Jesus' farewell speech is a mix of three exhortatory elements: predictions, promises, and prescriptions:

Predictions: "You will be led astray" (13:5, 6, 22); "You will be handed over" (13:9, 11, 12); "You will be beaten" (13:9); "You will testify to authorities" (13:9); "You will be tried" (13:11); "You will be hated" (13:13); "You will perceive incomparable tribulation" (13:19).

Promises: "God rules the chaos" (13:7); "The end will come" (13:7); "The gospel must be proclaimed everywhere" (13:10); "The Holy Spirit will be given and will speak" (13:11); "The one who endures will be saved" (13:13); "The Lord has cut short those days of tribulation for the elect" (13:20); "I have told you everything" (13:23); "You will see the Son of Man come" (13:26); "The Son of Man will gather his elect" (13:27); "You will perceive and know the time" (13:29); "My words will never pass away" (13:31).

Prescriptions: "Be able to see" (13:5, 9, 23, 33); "Don't be alarmed" (13:7); "Don't worry" (13:11); "Pray" (13:18); "Don't be fooled by falsehood" (13:21); "Learn" (13:28); "Keep alert" (13:33); "Steward your work" (13:34); "Keep watch" (13:34, 35, 37); "Don't be sleeping" (13:36).

The Character of Discipleship (13:5–37)

Rather than go through a verse-by-verse commentary on this complex, extended discourse, let us simply try to sketch the character of Christian discipleship as painted for us by the Master, Jesus Christ.

A Matter of the Heart

A disciple of Jesus Christ should not be impressed by the superficial grandeur of institutional religion. This important characteristic of discipleship is often neglected in treatments of this text, but it is assuredly part of Jesus' concern. There may not be a more emphatically phrased declaration from Jesus' mouth than his response to the disciples' enchantment over the Temple's architecture in 13:2. As they exit for the last time, swooning to Jesus, "Look, Teacher, aren't these magnificent stones and magnificent buildings" (13:1), he sharply responds with two emphatic negatives, literally, "There's *never* going to be a single stone left upon another that *cannot ever* be torn down!" (13:2). Jesus is acutely aware how tempted his disciples are by the outward impressiveness of institutional religion, which boasts that externals like buildings, budgets, and bodies prove internal faithfulness. Here he firmly reminds his own that discipleship is measured by *intangibles,* a character that will not crumble nor be spent nor be gauged by popularity.

A Matter for Today

A disciple of Jesus Christ should not be preoccupied with details of the last days, but with faithful stewardship of *today.* To the disciples' plea for the When and the What of the last days, Jesus responds with the "See" and the "Don't be alarmed" of these days (13:5–7). Even in 13:32–33, when he explicitly answers their original question, his emphasis is upon the present when he says "See" and "Keep alert." Disciples of Jesus Christ are not to be easily sensationalized by the

"Wars and rumors of wars"

coming events of heaven because they should be resolutely focused on the current events of earth. Williamson (241) highlights the risk of detachment when Christians specialize in eschatology: "Besides pretending to know more than the Son does, date fixers often have little sense of responsibility for the world, whose destruction they await with fascinated detachment."

In this final lecture, Jesus is concerned that the disciples will project God's reign on earth into the future—reserving it for the events at the end of the age—and mistake God's rule here and now, today. He has lived with these disciples and is acquainted with their propensity to arrange life by the clock's tick (human-centered *chronos*) rather than by divine timing (God-centered *kairos,* 13:33). Jesus wants disciples free from the tyranny of linear time and available for God's intervention whenever and wherever and however God chooses. Moreover, he wants the disciples' feet firmly planted on this earth, not leap-frogging vainly onto the new earth which is to come. Responsible disciples take the here-and-now seriously because they understand that the here-and-now is the sovereign domain of their Maker.

> "In contrast to [those fascinated with pinpointing a date], the Marcan Jesus speaks of responsibilities imposed by the master who left us in charge here."—Williamson, *Mark,* Interpretation, 241.

A Matter of Clear-Sightedness

A disciple of Jesus Christ should emphasize discernment above knowledge. Said another way, for a disciple of Jesus Christ knowledge *is* discernment, the grace-filled capacity to see clearly. Perhaps the most remarkable dimension of this speech is Jesus' lack of concern for the content of his disciples' faith and his overwhelming concern for the *depth of their perception.* Jesus seems almost obsessed with his disciples' vulnerability to falsehood. He cautions that folk—*Christian folk!*—will try to lead them astray with their false messianic claims (13:6, 21) and that pseudo-christs and pseudo-prophets will try to seduce them with their magic (13:22). Once again, we appreciate that discipleship for Jesus is much more *a way of seeing* than it is an accumulation of facts or doctrines. That's why Jesus saturates this speech with verbs of perception: "see" (13:5, 9, 23, 33); "perceive" (13:14, 29); "discern" (13:14); "observe" (13:26); "ascertain" (13:28); "recognize" (13:28, 29); "alert" (13:33); and "watch" (13:34, 35, 37). When it comes to the substance of knowledge, Jesus emphasizes that the disciples *already have* all that they need, "I have already told you everything" (13:23, NRSV), or he assures them that they *will be given* all that they need in the moment of crisis, "Say whatever is given you at that moment, for it is not you who speak, but the Holy Spirit" (13:11). Disciples are to distinguish the authentic from the artificial.

A Matter of Ultimate Trust

A disciple of Jesus Christ should see God reigning in the midst of earth's tribulation and know that God is sovereign. That's why disciples are not surprised by the convulsions of God's creation, because they trust that God is always in the tribulation, sovereignly giving birth (birth pangs, 13:8). This explains how Jesus can lace his description of world conflict with words of comfort. There will be war, international and intercontinental conflict, earthquakes, famines (13:7–8), absolutely unprecedented tribulation (13:19), cosmic collapse (13:24–25)—even the disappearance of reality as we know it (13:31)—yet the disciple of Jesus Christ can discern and rest in God's sovereign rule. He or she will reliably suppress the anxiety (13:7, 11) that

> "In the midst of upheaval and suffering, people often fear that God is not present, that God has abandoned them, that history is random after all. Mark's Jesus seeks to quell such fear by assuring followers beforehand that God is present and at work even in the midst of suffering."—Mitzi Minor, *The Spirituality of Mark*, 68.

either God or God's people is in any long-term jeopardy. A disciple of Jesus Christ seeks to trust God's covenantal care when the tribulation is most severe. This is why Jesus invokes Israel's covenantal self-understanding ("the elect") three times right when his description of creation's birth pangs becomes most intense (13:20, 22, 27); he is reassuring the church that, despite appearances, God still rules the world. Disciples are characterized by a profound appreciation for God's providence (Jesus employs the "verb of providential necessity," *deo,* three times in 13:7, 10, 14).

A Matter of Focused Perseverance

A disciple of Jesus Christ should focus on the essential mission of the church, come hell or high water. In fact, hell and high water are sure bets for disciples, but these must not deter or distract disciples from the mission to which they have been called. This mission has been consistently defined throughout Mark's Gospel as the sowing of the glad tidings of God's earthly reign in Jesus Christ and the combat against evil in God's creation (3:14–15). Nothing should distract or detract or derail disciples from their apostolic calling. Neither betrayal, physical abuse, nor political tyranny (13:11), nor family division (13:12), nor public persecution (13:13) will be able to stop disciples from testifying before principalities and

> "Mark 13 speaks to those who expect too much and to those who expect too little. It is especially pertinent for those who have forgotten to expect anything at all."—Williamson, *Mark*, Interpretation, 243.

powers (13:9), and proclaiming to all nations (13:10) the glad tidings of God's gracious rule in Jesus Christ. Disciples of Jesus Christ will be like slaves in charge, tenaciously tending to their work; and like doorkeepers, humbly obeying their command to keep watch while the lord of the house has gone on a journey (13:34–35). Disciples will be characterized by their steadfast endurance to the end (13:13).

A Matter of Humility

A disciple of Jesus Christ is humble. Humility may just be the hallmark of Christian character in the New Testament. We hear Jesus emphasize this in his farewell speech in several places. A disciple is not self-reliant, but critically dependent upon the Holy Spirit (13:11); a disciple trusts in the adequacy of the "already" and does not desperately or arrogantly grasp for more (13:23); a disciple does not attempt to wrest control from God, but relies on God's capacity to fulfill whatever is promised (13:30–31); and a disciple is content *not* to know what only God knows (13:32, 33, 35). Authentic disciples must suppress their ego-need to possess the high seat in the hall of eternal secrets. The church should be unembarrassed to have been appointed slave and butler for the Lord of the universe.

In the end, the characterization of chapter 13 as apocalyptic literature is misleading. In Mark's hands, what may once have been apocalyptic traditions about Jesus and the end of time have been transformed into traditions about the kingdom of God. Apocalyptic literature and kingdom of God literature differ in highly significant ways. In *The Interpreter's Dictionary of the Bible,* Martin Rist describes apocalyptic literature as generally pessimistic about the present age of human history, because the present age and the world as we know it have been entirely forfeited to Satan. Since the world is not redeemable, as such, human beings have little role to play. "Everything awaits God's expected intervention" (*Rist,* 161). When apocalypticism is understood thus, the thirteenth chapter of Mark roundly resists being construed as traditional apocalyptic literature.

> "Apocalypse is meant to bring us to our senses, allowing us a sobering, and usually painful, glimpse of what is possible in the new life we build from the ashes of the old."—Kathleen Norris, *Amazing Grace: A Vocabulary of Faith* (New York: Riverhead Books, 1998), 321.

In contrast to apocalyptic literature, kingdom of God literature is impenetrably optimistic, emphasizing that the world as we know it and the present age of human history actually constitute the physical and spiritual kingdom in which God reigns supreme, Satan's activity notwithstanding. Moreover, God's people are citizens of the kingdom and empowered by God to be agents of redemptive change within the kingdom. Clearly, these emphases are much more consistent with the nature of chapter 13 and the whole trajectory of the Gospel of Mark. The keynote of Mark's theology—"The time has been fulfilled, and the kingdom of God has come near" (1:15)—sounds his overwhelming conviction that, in the person of Jesus Christ, God has *already* intervened in the world as we know it and is actively present transforming this present age of history. Mark believes this is the occasion not merely for optimism, but for gladness and joy; it is the season not for apathy toward the world, but for peaceful, urgent, and untiring discipleship.

So we see that Jesus' bewildering Little Apocalypse is actually a comforting word of hope about the kingdom of God come to earth. His purpose is to consolidate the faith of his disciples on the eve of his departure. How distraught Jesus would be to learn that we had ever reduced this inspirational last sermon on the (Temple) mount to a repository for boring, eschatological details. The treasures contained herein are not meant to be stashed away for the future, but are to be spent straightaway to "strengthen discipleship in the present," to "arm us against the wiles of deceivers," to "sustain us in whatever suffering or persecution we must endure," to "motivate us to get on with preaching the gospel," and to "ennoble and relativize the common round of daily life by making each moment subject to the invasion of the Son of Humanity" (Williamson, 243).

> ## Want to Know More?
>
> **About apocalyptic literature and the Last Days?** See William Barclay, *At the Last Trumpet: Jesus Christ and the End of Time* (Louisville, Ky.: Westminster John Knox Press, 1998), 1–17, 85–93.
>
> **About the significance of the Temple?** See R. E. Clements, *Jeremiah* (Atlanta: John Knox Press, 1988), 43–45; for a thorough and technical discussion, see Horst Dietrich Preuss, *Old Testament Theology*, vol. 2, Old Testament Library (Louisville, Ky.: Westminster John Knox Press, 1996), 39–51.

Questions for Reflection

1. A theme of this whole Gospel has been to keep awake or alert. What has Jesus meant by this command? How and why are the faithful to keep awake?
2. Another theme of the Gospel has been the sense that God (or the Father) is the one who is in control. How does this passage (Mark 13) illustrate the power and providence of God?

3. Some of the signs of the last times are described in verses 7–8. Since wars and earthquakes have been happening for centuries, how do you reconcile these statements with your experience of the end not happening?

4. Mark 13:35 not only continues the theme of watchfulness in the Gospel, it foreshadows some of the forthcoming events. Knowing the rest of the Gospel, what connective points do you see between this verse and the passion and resurrection of Jesus (Mark 14:32–16:2)?

The Mystery Forsaken

Lest there linger any doubt that the integrity of discipleship rests solely on the goodness and mercy of Jesus Christ and not on the valor of our labor, Mark brings us the crash of Peter. In one scene with two acts, Mark takes our breath away in a contrast of character between Jesus Christ and the disciple Peter.

Jesus stands on trial before the Jewish Council and Peter stands on trial before a slave girl. Like diamond and sandstone, Mark tumbles master and disciple together. One increases in brilliance; the other disintegrates before our eyes. Williamson (267) argues that these two character sketches "relate to each other like twin stars"—"the movement of each . . . is best understood in terms of the counterforce of the other." This is literature's quintessential scene of courage and cowardice.

In our last passage—Jesus' farewell address (13:1–37)—we suggested that Mark shifted the mode of Jesus' speech in order to stun us with the urgency of the church's mission. While Jesus' speech was full of terrifying apocalyptic imagery, Jesus' motive was to convey hope to struggling disciples, not to frighten them to death as some preachers are wont to do with his words. From 8:27 onward, Mark de-emphasizes Jesus' ministry to nondisciples while emphasizing his ministry to the Twelve. Jesus has been preparing them for his departure.

In all such preparatory moments, there is a temptation to turn inward to gird oneself. Mark is well-acquainted with those in his congregation who have transformed Jesus' grace-filled imperatives of self-denial and cross bearing into a platform for the disciple-of-the-month award. Perhaps Mark himself has fallen prey to the error that discipleship is a matter of enlightened self-exertion, and has painfully returned outside of himself to the radiant sunshine of grace.

Mark has marinated this scene of courage and cowardice to heighten its pathos. Back in the Garden of Gethsemane just verses ago, Jesus is forthright about the disciples' lack of internal capacity, buttressing his prediction of their failure by quoting the prophet Zechariah: "You will all become deserters; for it is written, 'I will strike the shepherd, and the sheep will be scattered'" (Mark 14:27, NRSV). Once again Peter jumps his master, insisting (as we disciples relentlessly insist) that he is not like the others. "Even though all become deserters, I will not" (14:29, NRSV). Jesus lays it down for Peter with embarrassing starkness: "Truly I tell you, this day, this very night, before the cock crows twice, you will deny me three times, Peter" (14:30, NRSV). But Peter only vehemently increases the noise, for he cannot handle this image of his inadequacy. "Even though I must die with you, *I will not deny you*" (14:31, NRSV, emphasis added). Peter speaks with such passion that he seduces the whole lot, for Mark tells us that "all of them said the same" (14:31, NRSV).

But the disciples' words fail to measure their action, for immediately upon Jesus' arrest later that night, Mark chillingly relates that "all of them deserted him and fled" (14:50, NRSV).

Williamson (263) sees this double strand of courage and cowardice as Mark's proclamation of the gospel in a nutshell, "how God deals with the sins of humankind." Williamson alerts us to be on the lookout here for the mysterious healing encounter between God's fidelity and our infidelity. Were the apostle Paul to see Mark's text, he might observe that Mark is urging us to behold him who knew no sin scandalously being made to be sin, so that in him we might become the righteousness of God (2 Cor. 5:21). If we do not experience a clash of despair and joy while reading this text, we might be reading it at too safe a distance.

As usual, Mark will not allow us to forget where we are in this drama. As chapter 14 opens, he immediately locates us precisely "two days before the Passover and the festival of Unleavened Bread" (14:1, NRSV). We are standing within the penumbra of the cross. What's more, Mark tells us that the teeth of evil have been sharpened for Jesus' death. His mere arrest no longer satisfies the establishment, but has become simply the first stage of his murder: "The chief priests and the scribes were looking for a way to arrest Jesus by stealth and *kill* him" (14:1, NRSV, emphasis added). Jesus' radical teaching about the Messiah—"that the Son of Humanity must . . . be *killed*" (8:31), that "they will *kill* him" (9:31), that "they will mock him, and spit upon him, and flog him, and *kill* him" (10:34, NRSV, emphasis added)— gapes before us, like the jaws of hell.

Since locating us two days before the Jewish feast of freedom in 14:1–2, Mark renders the events of the next few hours with an ominous tone. Before we recognize it, Mark has us in Jesus' funeral procession:

- Jesus is anointed by a woman in a leper's kitchen (14:3–9).
- Judas conspires with the religious authorities (14:10–11).
- Jesus celebrates a final Passover Seder with his beloved (14:12–25).
- Jesus predicts his total desertion; Peter vehemently rebuts (14:26–31).
- Jesus admonishes his disciples to remain awake, praying that they not be led into trial (14:32–42).
- Judas kisses Jesus good-bye; the disciples flee (14:43–52).

The Prelude (14:53–54)

Mark establishes the tone of this drama by noting at the outset that Jesus is *taken* and that Peter *follows*. Mark teases us with the irony: Jesus is not in control of his destiny, but remains free; Peter is in control, but is bound. Peter plays it safe and follows at a distance.

But why? What is Peter's motive? Does he follow for Jesus' sake or for Peter's? Does he follow out of compassion or does he follow to prove Jesus wrong in his prediction? Is Peter risking his life for Jesus' sake, stealing his way "right into the courtyard" and to fireside "with the guards" (14:54)? Or, is Peter risking Jesus' life for Peter's sake? What a delicious space in the narrative inviting the church's interpretation!

The Profile of Courage (14:55–65)

As if to build a foundation beneath us, to help us recover from our failure, Mark first weaves the profile of courage: Jesus Christ on trial by the upholders of the whole religious status quo. This is the moment of truth for the ecclesiastical establishment; they have stealthily assembled themselves in the heat of the night. Everything has been choreographed. Jesus will be tried on two charges, treason (14:58) and blasphemy (14:61–62). When he is found guilty, this establishment will turn him over to Rome and force capital punishment. The alliance between synagogue and state has a deathly cast.

> "No genuine inquiry into the claims of Jesus, this 'trial' is, rather, the rejection of those claims by the official leaders of Judaism, corresponding to the rejection of Christian claims about Jesus at the time this Gospel was written."—Williamson, *Mark,* Interpretation, 264.

But wait, something is awry. The theo-political machinery is halting. Mark carefully uses a tense (the Greek imperfect tense) to paint a picture of *repeated* action by the religious prosecutors. As he does so, the scene devolves into a mockery of justice, where the official authorizers abdicate all relationship with truth. So severe is their abdication that it becomes a comic tragedy. Here's the scene, literally, in its grievous hilarity (14:55–59):

> The whole council *was searching* for testimony against Jesus, but they *were not finding.* So many *were giving* false testimony against Jesus, but their testimony *conflicted.* So some stood up and *continued to give* false testimony against Jesus . . . but even on this point their testimony *conflicted.*

Mark parodies these religious professionals and reveals their authority to be entirely self-generated. They do not have a case, so they fabricate a case. But they lack the authority even to fabricate! They are desperate, bumbling, and self-aggrandizing, and before them Jesus stands in silent grandeur. Their charge against Jesus is treason, but they perjure themselves, charging Jesus with a self-reference he never made. Presumably, their charge is based on Jesus' vague but forthright prediction of the Temple's destruction in 13:2. But because they fear him, they restate Jesus' words as if he were personally claiming to be the agent of the Temple's destruction.

They break the ninth commandment—bearing false witness against Jesus—and everyone knows it. But there the accusation hangs, thinner than the air in which it is suspended. And there Jesus stands, in peaceful stillness.

The high priest cannot stomach the spectacle in his courtroom, so he jumps up and asks Jesus, "Have you no answer to this charade? What is it that they testify against you?" The high priest seems suspended in disbelief over the folly of the accusers and the silence of the accused. The reader senses the discord within the high priest: "Since there is obviously no just charge against you, then why in the world don't you say something? Defend yourself! Just give me one tiny word on which to hang your acquittal!"

Right here, the church simply must stop and gaze in awe at Jesus' courage. Within the hollow chambers of our modern obsession with individual rights and self-determination, Jesus' silence reverberates. Jesus has no need to defend the truth in words, for he has already defended it in his whole person. Jesus rests securely in the hands of God, like one who can sleep peacefully through a storm at sea (4:38). His silence is not a mere legal strategy, but his faith in action. He is unafraid of death and has no personal need to mount an oral defense of the truth. Jesus will serve neither the need of the high priest nor the need of the reader for unnecessary words. Jesus' defense of silence accomplishes volumes more than any wordy cry for justice.

So the high priest changes tack, discards the effort to convict Jesus of treason, and raises the second charge of blasphemy asking, "Are you really and truly the Christ of God?" (14:61). Intriguingly, at this critical *theological* juncture Jesus now breaks the silence. However, if we construe his response—"I am"—as a simple affirmation to the high priest that he is the Messiah, we will miss the startling profundity of Jesus' profession.

> "And now, with the drama of his passion already underway, when there is no longer any possibility for popular misunderstanding of the meaning of his claim, Jesus answers unequivocally: 'I am.'"—Williamson, *Mark*, Interpretation, 265.

As noted in our previous discussion of Exodus 3 in unit 6, when Jesus used that text to strategically refute the Sadducees (Mark 12:18–27), there is no story in the Hebrew scripture as central to Judaism as the "burning bush" story. This is the story of the Self-disclosure of God's proper name to Moses, and with it, the disclosure of the character and power of the Holy One of Israel. This huge moment in the Bible is worth quoting:

¹³But Moses said to God, "If I come to the Israelites and say to them, 'The God of your ancestors has sent me to you,' and they ask me, 'What is his name?' what shall I say to them?"

¹⁴God said to Moses, "I AM [or I WILL BE] WHO I AM [or WHO I WILL BE]." God said further, "Thus you shall say to the Israelites, 'I AM [I WILL BE] has sent me to you.' "

¹⁵God also said to Moses, "Thus you shall say to the Israelites, 'YHWH, the God of your ancestors, the God of Abraham, the God of Isaac, and the God of Jacob, has sent me to you': This is my name forever, and this my title for all generations." (Ex. 3:13–15, NRSV alt.)

Many people do not realize that the God of Israel has a proper name. The proper name of God consists of four Hebrew consonants, YHWH, revealed to Moses that day out of the burning bush. These four consonants are called the "Tetragrammaton" (literally, four-lettered) and they constitute the most sacred of Hebrew words, considered to this day absolutely unutterable by observant Jews of all traditions. (The word *adonai,* or lord, is substituted for it in reading or translation.) While the name YHWH is essentially untranslatable, it is very similar in form to the ordinary Hebrew verb "to be" (*hayah*), which can also be translated "will be" depending on the understanding of the tense. Indeed, as we see above in Exodus 3, it is no less than God who closely associates "his" name YHWH with the verb "to be" in Exodus 3:14. Responsible English translations will let us know whenever the holy Hebrew Tetragrammaton is present by capitalizing the reference to LORD.

"The blindfolding suggests that those in charge of the prisoner played a malicious game of blindman's bluff, in which Jesus was the victim."—Hare, *Mark,* Westminster Bible Companion, 202.

When the high priest asks Jesus, "Are you the Messiah, the Son of the Blessed One?" (Mark 14:61, NRSV) and Jesus responds, "I AM," he invokes the proper name of the Lord of Israel, and with it, the divine persona and its incumbent majesty and power. This is not a laughing matter for the high Jewish court. Jesus, Mary and Joseph's oldest boy—the woodworker from Nazareth—is personally assuming the Holy Identity! It is the last straw.

No wonder the high priest tears his clothes and screams, "Blasphemy!" No wonder the whole Sanhedrin unanimously votes for the cross. No wonder some of the Jewish leaders begin to spit, some to blindfold, some to slap, some to ridicule. No wonder even the Roman guards join in and beat him.

The Profile of Cowardice (14:66–72)

As Jesus stands inside before the high priest, Peter sits outside before the high priest's slave girl. We know nothing about Peter's motive; we know only that he is warming himself at the fire (14:54, 67). Because he stole there "at a distance" and is sitting with the guards, we detect timidity. Or is it shrewdness? Or could it be courage? Why has he followed? Why does he mingle? What could he possibly wish to accomplish? We are hopeful.

When the slave girl sees Peter, she stares at him (14:67). Why? What is it about Peter that draws her? Is she, surely a Jewess, drawn to his Jewishness amidst the Roman guard? Is it his migrant dress? Is there something about his countenance in the fire's glow? She stares. We are still hopeful.

Then she identifies. She identifies Peter, and she identifies Jesus. She identifies Peter by his association with Jesus, and she identifies Jesus by his hometown, Nazareth. While it is not evident in English translations, she pointedly identifies Peter as one who continued to hang around Jesus, "Hey you, you were formerly associated with Jesus." Does she whisper? Or accuse? Is she sympathetic? Or severe?

We do not know. Does Peter himself know? Perhaps Peter does not care, for he quickly denies her identification. And he denies her with tremendous force. Mark did not have to preserve it this way for the church generations later. In fact, Mark could have softened Peter's infidelity and made his character more presentable as the representative churchman. But Mark preserves Peter's lie with all its brute deception.

Peter makes two confessions to the slave girl (14:68). A single confession would have been sufficient. But Peter chooses to be emphatic. He declares that he has not been associated with Jesus of Nazareth by using two distinct Greek tenses and two different Greek verbs. He could not have been more emphatic.

First, he denies Jesus; then he denies the slave girl. He denies having known Jesus; then he denies comprehending the slave girl's meaning. He denies Jesus with

Want to Know More?

About the requirements of Jewish trial law? See Barclay, *The Gospel of Mark*, Daily Study Bible, 349–50.

About God's name? See James D. Newsome, *Exodus*, Interpretation Bible Studies (Louisville, Ky.: Geneva Press, 1998), 18–19.

About blasphemy? See George Arthur Buttrick, ed., *The Interpreter's Dictionary of the Bible*, vol. A–D (Nashville: Abingdon Press, 1962), 445.

the Greek perfect tense, then he denies the slave girl with the simple Greek present tense. A nuance of the Greek perfect tense is that it indicates *an action begun in the past whose force continues into the present.* Thus, Peter's first denial of Jesus sounded something like this:

> I have *not ever* known Jesus,
> nor do I even comprehend what you, madam, are saying.

Peter lies about Jesus, and he lies to the slave girl of the high priest. He abandons the one and insults the other. He could not be more deceitful. He departs her company, but remains within earshot of the cock's crow.

Later, the slave girl catches sight of Peter again (14:69–70a). This time, perhaps irritated by his earlier deception, she begins identifying Peter publicly, "This man is one of them" (14:70, NRSV). Curiously, her first "make" on Peter is his association with Jesus while her second is his association with Jesus' disciples. What this tells us is that Jesus' disciples had become a known entity and—with Jesus' arrest and conviction—an entity with social liability. How liable is it to be a Christian today?

This second time around, Mark does not give us Peter's response, but he tells us that Peter was making an ongoing effort to perpetuate the deceit (this is the power of the Greek imperfect tense). Mark hands us this simple, stark snapshot of Peter: "He continued to deny."

By the time the third denial rolls around a little while later, the slave girl's public identification of Peter has taken root in the crowd (14:70b–71). His association with the disciples of Jesus has grown into a public matter, in particular because something about his Galilean upbringing—face? accent? dress?—makes him stand out here in Jerusalem. The make on Peter has crescendoed. There is now no anonymity. "You are truly a disciple, because you're Galilean!" (v. 70). Peter has become a celebrity.

For Peter, this is the last straw. He breaks. Mark tells us that Peter becomes hostile and foul, cursing and vowing this third and final denial. In the ancient world, cursing was a theological act, in which the curser literally called down the wrath of God. This is the meaning of the Greek verb used here, *anathematizo,* from which we transliterate our "anathematize," which means "to proclaim a formal damning." As if cursing is insufficient, Peter adds a vow (to God) for emphasis! The extreme severity of Peter's third denial (14:71) angrily leaps out at us and Mark does not tame it:

> *God damn it!*
> I *swear* (to God),
> I have *never known* this man you're talking about!

Peter's singular, overwhelming concern in this moment is to completely disassociate himself from Jesus Christ. He renounces Jesus Christ as vehemently as one could in the ancient world. And the rest is history.

A shrill crowing pierces the night. And a memory slays Peter dead in his tracks. With an unusual intransitive use of the Greek verb that means "breaking in" (compare 4:37), Mark leaves Peter collapsed in our arms (14:72), literally:

> And having broken in(side),
> he was weeping.

Thus Mark concludes his comparison of character between the Master and the disciple. He has fashioned the quintessential scene of courage and cowardice. We conclude in the same way we opened this unit. Mark has brought us the crash of Peter in case there lingers any doubt that the integrity of discipleship rests solely on the goodness and mercy of Jesus Christ, and not on the valor of our labor. Williamson (267) embraces Mark's open-ended conclusion: "Peter's unresolved guilt functions as an implicit appeal to the reader to try to do better than Peter. More profoundly, it depicts the human condition. If in Jesus we see how God always is, in Peter we see how we always are."

> "Protesting innocence, Peter is convicted by the narrative as guilty. Convicted as guilty and deserving death, Jesus is proclaimed by the narrative to be innocent, just, and ultimately victorious."—Williamson, *Mark*, Interpretation, 267.

Yes! The church is called by Jesus Christ to deny itself, to raise its cross, and to follow behind him.

No! The church will ultimately affirm itself, lay down its cross, and angrily deny Jesus Christ.

"At a deeper level," Williamson continues (268),

> the text proclaims the gospel. The dark side of the message is that we do not follow Jesus, despite our high intentions and loud protestations;

but, like Peter, we in fact deny him. The good news is that our salvation depends not on our petty performance, but on the faithfulness of God. Jesus' firm "I am" evokes a God who is in the dock; who, in subjecting himself to our judgment, judges us; who, not sparing his own Son but giving him up for us all, redeems even those who deny him; who, from most unlikely material, builds a church, a temple not made with hands; whose power is made perfect in weakness and whose ultimate vindication is as sure as are past fulfillments of his word.

Here Jesus himself predicts the denial of all Christian disciples. Yet Jesus himself continues to call the church to its task, "chasing us with goodness and mercy all the days of our lives"(Ps. 23:6). This is evident because the next mention of Peter in Mark's Gospel happens to be made by a young man dressed in white sitting in Jesus' empty tomb:

> "Peter's sorry tale is included in the Gospels as a classic instance of the superabundance of God's grace."—Hare, *Mark*, Westminster Bible Companion, 204.

> Do not be alarmed;
> you are looking for Jesus of Nazareth, who was crucified.
> He has been raised; he is not here.
> Look, there is the place they laid him.
> But go, tell his disciples *and Peter.*

(Mark 16:6–7, NRSV, emphasis added)

And we will dwell in the house of the LORD forever.

? Questions for Reflection

1. After Jesus' arrest, Peter follows him. This unit asks about Peter's motives. Why do you think Peter followed Jesus into the courtyard (14:54)? How might you have responded if you had stood in Peter's place?
2. The events of Jesus' trial are shown to be a mockery. The charges cannot be substantiated. But there is a sense in which Jesus is always on trial. What are some of the questions, charges, and doubts by which Jesus stands on trial today?
3. This unit states, "Jesus has no need to defend the truth in words, for he has already defended the truth in his whole person." Do you

agree or disagree with this statement? Why or why not? Is this an absolute? Are there times when the truth needs to be defended with words? When are those times?

4. The whole Gospel of Mark is fraught with irony, but it is particularly noticeable in the passion and trial narrative. When the cock crows during Peter's denial, what does that communicate? Why does a rooster crow? Peter curses and takes a sacred oath that he does not know Jesus, and then a new day is signaled. Think about some of the ironies of this new day. What events will now transpire? What events are finished and cannot be undone? What opportunities and choices lie ahead? Where do you find yourself in this story?

9 Mark 15:16–41

The Mystery Solved

We know this story. It is, deservedly, the most widely known story in the world. But as familiar as it is, the story of the crucifixion never becomes too familiar. We plumb its depths year after year, yet its riches remain abundant.

This story haunts us. We never fully believe it; we are not able. Unlike the story of the nativity, the story of the cross implicates us. On the day Jesus was born, we just sat by and received the marvelous news. Even if we were the innkeeper, we simply apologized and showed them out back. We had nothing else to do with it. "The fullness of time had come," Paul concludes (Gal. 4:4, NRSV).

But on the afternoon Jesus died, at exactly 3:00 P.M., after three hours of sustained darkness, we are wrenched with guilt, as deeply as if we had swung the Roman mallet. Of course we did not, nor did we stop those who did, for we had already committed our abandonment. No, this was no manger to which we scurried with gifts; this was an execution chamber in which we extinguished the Gift.

We had everything to do with the death of Jesus Christ. And we still do. Knowing this mysteriously

"When it was noon, darkness came over the whole land."

cleanses us and grounds our freedom. We have placed Jesus' horrifying end at the center of the Apostles' Creed, to sound a reverberating death knell for innocence: "Suffered, crucified, dead, buried, descended." If we fail to come to grips with our complicity in this dark center of human existence, we will not comprehend our salvation. Only upon our owning the cross can the great, glad tidings that have been pealing our liberty all along begin to be heard.

That is the eternal power of this story.

An Overview

Mark's narrative of Peter's denial in 14:66–72 comes as close as any narrative can to preparing us for the crucifixion of Jesus Christ. There Mark cast the disciples' withdrawal from Jesus in the form of Peter's denial. Ever the spokesman for the disciples, Peter served as the test case for the disciples' faithfulness. And he failed. Every last one of the Twelve is gone from the stage.

Mark now proceeds in his narrative of the cross to remove everyone else from the company of Jesus. Mark's account of the crucifixion is a litany of abandonment, in which he vividly portrays the aloneness of Jesus in his death. With crescendo, this story unfolds the despair of a world and its Savior completely at odds. "The failure of his disciples through misunderstanding, betrayal, denial, and flight reaches its nadir at the cross . . . not a single disciple is present. The abandonment of Jesus . . . reaches its climax" (Williamson, 276–77).

Though Jesus' engagement with the Roman procurator, Pontius Pilate, is an important scene in Mark's drama, we

> "Were you there when they crucified my Lord?" In the Gospel of Mark, sadly, the response is "No."

will restrict our focus to the crucifixion proper, taking as our starting point Mark's eerie signal in 15:15, "After flogging Jesus, Pilate handed him over to be crucified." We take 15:41 as Mark's conclusion of the crucifixion proper, for in the next verse evening arrives, officially ending this day of days.

What immediately strikes us in Mark's crucifixion narrative is how jammed it is with ridicule. Every figure surrounding Jesus here at the end—with the exception of God and the women—can be construed as mocking Jesus. Through it all, the defendant remains silent. As

Mark tells it, Jesus has only one word remaining. He will save it for the end. He has completely surrendered his fate to other hands.

This scene is a paradigm for nonviolence. Christ's refusal to retaliate or to defend himself in the slightest against this legal debauchery makes a sham of much ecclesiastical protest. The church would be well-served to know this defining story more deeply.

Abandonment by Rome (15:16–28)

As if the miscarriage of justice in the capital sentence of the Messiah is not glaring enough, Mark proceeds to fill Jesus' final moments with ugliness beyond imagination. And it is no wonder that the Messiah crucified is such "a stumbling block to Jews and foolishness to Gentiles" (1 Cor. 1:23, NRSV). Jesus is so meek! Whatever is thrown at him, he just receives without a word. How can such a man possibly have any association with the mighty power and eternal mind of God? Pilate's abdication of Jesus' punishment to the mob and Pilate's own farewell lashing of Jesus should have satisfied even the foulest lust. He could then have respectfully passed Jesus to the guards, and we could have been done with this heinous scene.

But no. Even the Roman soldiers—stagehands who in no way stand to benefit from Jesus' humiliation—have plotted their little ritual of insult. What is it about Jesus Christ that elicits such vengeance? He is a "dead man walking" and the prison guards are poking fun down the runway. They have obviously planned this, for they summon the whole cohort to the spectacle (15:16). They are a fraternity whose identity depends on others' awareness of their authority. They must display their muscle, even when it is ridiculous.

So the soldiers costume and salute Jesus as they would the Caesar, "Hail to thee, O King of Israel of the lineage of David!" (15:18). Perhaps these Romans have longed to lampoon Jewish beliefs and customs, and this thoroughly humiliated Jew provides their release. The irony of this whole scene is sublime, and we should not overlook it. We are witness to an alliance between ideological enemies—monotheistic Jews and Caesar-worshiping Romans—for carrying out the death sentence of the Prince of Peace.

As Mark pictures it, the police circle the hostage king, whipping his head with reeds, spitting on him, and faking his worship. It does not last long, but the scene is preposterous. As they near the main street, the soldiers shrewdly remove from Jesus anything that might suggest royalty to the Jewish mob. Having fulfilled their obligation to the fraternity, the soldiers resume their professionalism. While not visible in the English, Mark shifts the whole drama at this moment into the more vivid Greek "historical present" tense: "They lead him out to crucify . . . They compel a passerby . . . They bring Jesus to Golgotha" (15:20–22).

Obviously, Jesus is not going to make it. So the soldiers arbitrarily grab a shopper to assist him. Many in the church have adored Simon of Cyrene for what they construe as a profound act of sympathy. How moviemakers love to portray Simon, initiating this act of noble charity! What we fail to appreciate is that Simon did not volunteer himself to the wilting Christ; he was insultingly plucked from the marketplace and forced at spearpoint to join a death march for convicts. Simon is not given any option. He is effectively compelled to help the convict onto the electric chair. This could only have been a huge embarrassment to Simon. We can be sure he wishes he had saved his errands in the city for another day.

> "Readers of Mark's story become spectators of the event—hostile, indifferent, or irresistibly drawn into the dramatic action."—Hare, *Mark*, Westminster Bible Companion, 214.

They march Jesus to the scary place, where he refuses anesthesia. "And they crucify him, and divide his clothes" (15:24).

That's it? We hardly felt it! The Roman guard dispenses the crucifixion like a mere vaccination. They push the dreaded button and then start bargaining for his belongings, as if they are at a yard sale.

No other Gospel renders this central moment in history more starkly. Somehow, Mark counters all instinct to embellish. This scene reveals more about God, humanity, and the future of the world than any other, and Mark gives us a stick figure! "This event, toward which Mark's entire story builds, is narrated in . . . just four words. . . . Why is it so powerful?" wonders Williamson (275).

Sure, Mark tells us the hour, he reminds us of the final mocking inscription, "The King of the Jews" (as much a mockery of the Jews as of Jesus), and he notes that two bandits were crucified alongside Jesus. But with Mark there is no last-minute forgiveness, no tenderness toward his mother and beloved John, no earthquake, no conversation with the robbers, no parched plea for water, no self-commission to the Father, no pronouncement of the end, no resurrection of the saints, no "seven last words."

Abandonment by Passersby, Jewish Leadership, and Fellow Crucified (15:29–32)

Following the Roman soldiers, Mark next brings to the stage a motley lot including Jerusalemites, chief priests, scribes, and the two bandits hanging alongside. This grouping by Mark widely spans class and respectability and demonstrates how ruthless Mark is in crafting Jesus' abandonment. The aloneness of Jesus Christ intensifies.

> "If ever people make a jest of our Christianity, it will help to remember that they did it to Jesus in a way that is worse than anything likely to happen to us."—Barclay, The Gospel of Mark, Daily Study Bible, 359.

What motive could "those passing by" (15:29) possibly have in hurling insults at Jesus upon the cross? Nonetheless, Mark tells us that complete strangers continued to hurl evil words at Jesus (the Greek word, *blasphemeo,* can be translated "blaspheme"). They are even violently wagging their heads for emphasis, "Well there he is, the Temple thrower-down and the three-day-rebuilder! How about rebuilding and throwing-down yourself from the cross!" The picture is a ruthless glimpse into our own propensity to behave like a mob.

To make sure we appreciate that mobbishness is not a practice in which only ordinary passersby engage, Mark relates that the religious leaders of Jerusalem—the Holy City's clergymen—are next in line (15:31–32). Like the head-waggers, these holy men disparage Jesus, privately among themselves and publicly to Jesus. Imagine this, the Jerusalem clergy association cruelly mocks Jesus with the very testimony of his followers, "Others he saved; himself he is unable to save! The Messiah! The King of Israel! Let him come down from the cross now, so that we ourselves might see and trust!"

> "Jesus was crucified between two thieves. It was a symbol of his whole life that even at the end he companied with sinners."—Barclay, The Gospel of Mark, Daily Study Bible, 362.

Lastly, Mark brings to the stage the two justly condemned thieves hanging alongside Jesus, probably nailed to the same wooden matrix of cross. They, too, have the shamelessness to join in the cacophony of ridicule. Mark puts it starkly, "Those crucified with him kept reviling him" (15:32). No inspiring promise of Paradise for the guilty here.

Abandonment by God (15:33–38)

At this point, any light we have been carrying flickers out and we are ushered by Mark into the heart of darkness, the death of the Son of God. Mark signals this suffocating moment with three hours of darkness "over the whole earth" (15:33). We begin to see why the early church committed us to that offensive phrase "and he descended into hell" in the Apostles' Creed. We even begin to feel shame to have ever dared think about removing it.

The starkness of Mark's narrative is especially glaring in his portrayal of Jesus on the cross. The other Gospel writers hear a variety of last words of Jesus (from NRSV):

"Father, forgive them; for they do not know what they are doing." (Luke 23:34)
"Woman, here is your son. . . . Here is your mother." (John 19:26–27)
"Truly I tell you, today you will be with me in Paradise." (Luke 23:43)
"I am thirsty." (John 19:28)
"Father, into your hands I commend my spirit." (Luke 23:46)
"It is finished." (John 19:30)

But for Mark, there is only one word that is adequate for this crisis:

"My God, my God, why have you abandoned me?" (Mark 15:34)

Mark collapses all seven last words of Jesus into this one cry of absolute loneliness. By it, Mark means to say simply that Jesus died alone. Nobody on earth. Nobody in heaven. The most anonymous death imaginable. The death of a beggar woman under a bridge at the fall of the Hiroshima bomb becomes royal in comparison to the death of Jesus Christ. The scene lends a chilling accuracy to Friedrich Nietzsche's cynical assertion, "The word 'Christianity' is already a misunderstanding— in reality there has been only one Christian, and he died on the Cross."

Of course we know that Jesus' last word is not original, that he is quoting the opening verse of Psalm 22. But this does not help. We can argue until the sun burns out whether Jesus was more conscious of the lament in this psalm or the messianic allusion, whether he was emphasizing the solemn beginning of the psalm or the triumphal ending. We can argue whether Jesus meant what he cried or cried what he meant, whether he merely felt abandoned or actually was abandoned. We can even argue whether Jesus was crying as a theologian or as a victim, and whether his cry actually had an objective referent or pointed back to himself. We can argue and argue and argue.

But the truth is, this moment is infinitely beyond argument. This scene jams the human intellect. "The interpreter must first meditate carefully on text and art, then speak only as may be necessary" (Williamson, 280). The meaning of this moment must be left to the artists. What Mark is trying to communicate is a kind of knowing available only to the human spirit. All that can be said is that God tried and failed. And nobody cared.

Even the quarrel about Elijah that erupts upon mishearing Jesus' slurred Aramaic "Eloi" turns into mockery that ironically articulates the truth. The bystanders' words in 15:36 should not be translated "Wait" (NRSV), but more cynically, "Leave him by himself! Let us see whether Elijah will come take him down."

Want to Know More?

About Psalm 22? See Jerome F. D. Creach, *Psalms*, Interpretation Bible Studies (Louisville, Ky.: Geneva Press, 1998), 86–94.

About Elijah and messianic expectations? See George Arthur Buttrick, ed., *The Interpreter's Dictionary of the Bible*, Vol. E–J (Nashville: Abingdon Press, 1962), 90; Barclay, *The Gospel of Mark*, Daily Study Bible, 213.

Abandonment by the Centurion (15:39)

If portraying abandonment is Mark's primary aim in sketching the crucifixion, then having a centurion confess his faith in Jesus Christ is problematic. Though much ado is made about this Gentile's concluding declaration (15:39), his "confession" tidies up a dreadful scene and places a bow on it in a way that is uncharacteristic of Mark. We should have learned by now that Mark never leaves the church an easy way out of crisis. Moreover, Mark generally prefers to convey meaning less explicitly, relying on silence, suggestiveness, juxtaposition, irony, and other more subtle literary techniques. Mark does not need a Gentile believer here at the end; in fact, it could be argued that having such subverts his art. The canvas Mark has painted is totally dark. We are there, but we are standing in the darkness. The Gentile centurion may not be holding a candle for us.

Let's explore an interpretation that maintains the integrity of Mark's purpose, an interpretation in which the centurion does not overtly confess Jesus Christ, but mocks Jesus like the others. When we examine the centurion's statement more closely, we find that the literal Greek word order of his exclamation is, "Truly / this man / Son of God / was being!" Since biblical Greek, like Hebrew, has no punctuation, we are free to supply it interpretively. This time, we discover that the centurion uses the Greek imperfect tense for the Greek verb "to be." The imperfect tense is a form of the past tense connoting that the action in the past had an ongoing or repetitive quality to it. So, for instance, if we wish to emphasize that an athlete's completed effort was persistent, we might use the Greek imperfect tense to say, "She was running," which could also be rendered, "She kept running," or even translated inceptively, "She was trying to run."

The long and the short of it is that the Greek allows for the centurion's statement to be open for interpretation. The centurion, who stands directly facing Jesus when he breathes out for the last time, could just as well be rendering a more subdued verdict, "Surely, this man *was trying to be* the Son of God." Or he could be confused, "Surely, this man was being *the Son of God?*" Or the centurion could be possessed of cynicism like the other Romans, "Surely, this man *used to be* the Son of God." Or—like others in this litany of abandonment—he could be rendering a mocking verdict, "*Sure, this* man was being the *Son of God.*"

Abandonment by the Women (15:40–41)

Lastly, we come to the women. But even the women will get no heroic treatment by this interpreter, as so many others have given them. Here at the close of this tragic day, Mark tells us two things about the women: (1) they are watching Jesus die from a distance (2) they *used to* follow him and *used to* minister to him when he was in Galilee (the Greek imperfect tense again!).

The problem is, in this particular moment fidelity does not consist of what we *used to do* with Jesus or how we *used to minister* to him. Jesus is no longer in Galilee; he is in Jerusalem on a tree. Though they are at least still on stage, the women are off in the distance, neither following nor ministering.

Afterword

Mark's primary intention in telling the church of the crucifixion of Jesus Christ is to tell a story of abandonment. Mark is a pastor-theologian, and like all pastor-theologians he longs for his congregation to comprehend the incarnation, to grasp the degree to which God shares their plight of forsakenness. At the same time, Mark wants these professing disciples of Jesus Christ to face their own willingness to abandon God and one another. What better way to communicate these difficult truths about God and ourselves than to craft a scene of universal abandonment? This is Mark's art. And he provides little relief from it. Karl Barth, one of the greatest theologians in this century, once made an observation that could be characterized as Markan. "Rightly understood," Barth asserted, "there are no Christians: there is only the eternal opportunity of becoming Christians—an opportunity at once accessible and inaccessible to all" (Barth, 321).

> "His throne is a cross, his courtiers two robbers, and his public the enemies who kill him."—Williamson, *Mark,* Interpretation, 277.

This is not to say that Mark does not use irony in his narrative to communicate the truth of Jesus Christ for eyes that see. Of course we see the truth of Jesus' royalty, even as the soldiers mock his royalty; deep down, we know that they are actually enthroning him. Of course we see the truth of Jesus' weakness, even as the Jewish leaders mock his weakness; deep down, we know that they are actually describing his power. Of course we see the truth of Jesus' Messiahship, even as bystanders mock his Messiahship; deep down, we know that they are actually announcing the epiphany of Israel's Davidic king. And of course we see the truth of the centurion's confession and the faithfulness of the women's endurance, even if the centurion is mocking and the women remain distant; deep down, we know that they are all standing face-to-face with the Son of God.

But we see all this through irony, not in the face value of words. Of all the Gospel writers, Mark understands that there can be no true release if we are not acquainted with grief; and no lasting freedom if we do not taste guilt.

Mark knows that Friday remains the only meaningful passage to Sunday.

? Questions for Reflection

1. According to this unit, the passage describing the crucifixion reveals more about God, humanity, and the future of the world

than any other. Why? What is revealed in the crucifixion of Jesus?

2. Quite a reversal has occurred in the response to Jesus by others. Only a few chapters ago, crowds pressed in upon him, he bested the Jewish leaders, and he was hailed a Son of David. What has led to this reversal? How easy is it to sway a crowd or popular opinion? What makes the difference? Be creative for a moment. How might the story have been different? What details could have changed, and what would have been their outcome?

3. This unit raises the question of the motive of the centurion's statement. What do you think the centurion meant by his declaration in verse 39?

4. Mark's description of the crucifixion is slightly different than that given in the other Gospels. Compare this passage with Matthew 27:24–56; Luke 23:26–49; and John 19:16–30. What details are distinctly Mark's? How do those details help shape Mark's Gospel?

10 Mark 16:1–8

The Mystery Precedes

We have come to the ending. Or shall we say, the beginning? For as we have already noted in unit 6, what distinguishes the Gospels as literature is that they were written backward, from finish to start. Of course, the plot of many stories is written "backward," in the sense that the author knows how the story will finish and thus crafts the plot toward that end. The Gospels are no exception here. Clearly, Mark knows where the story is headed and writes in that direction. Literature is literature is literature.

"Very early, after the sun had risen . . . "

The Gospel story, however, is literature that is born (and reborn) in its ending. As a human cannot be said to exist apart from his or her birth, so the Gospel story cannot be said to exist apart from its ending. As there is organic continuity from birth to being for human life, there is organic continuity from *ending* to being for the Gospel story. Without its ending, the Gospel story lacks truthfulness; worse, it is entirely unimaginable.

The Peculiar Nature of the Gospel

When we say that the Gospel story is a story that has come into being "backward," we mean that it did not originate with its author—that it was a story that could not be created from a human vantage point—but that it was *given*. Mark neither could nor would have lifted a finger to tell this story had the life of Jesus Christ not ended as it did. There simply would have been no sensible impetus to continue remembering Jesus Christ.

Now what is true for the Gospel story is also true for the people who identify with the Gospel story, the church. A Christian existence would not be possible had the life of Jesus Christ not ended as it did. Thus it can be said that the peculiar nature of Christian life is that it is lived "backward," as the Christian story is written "backward." This is what Jesus is trying to teach Nicodemus in the third chapter of John's Gospel, that a Christian person is a person who is born "backward" from the resurrection, that a Christian existence is an existence that begins anew in its ending. Jesus is essentially teaching Nicodemus that a Christian life originates not with the person who lives it, but is given from above.

The Significance of the Resurrection

This is not to say that the *distinctiveness* of Christian theology and life lies in the ending of the story of Jesus' life. It does not. The way the Gospel story ends does not distinguish Christianity from other religions. As emphasized in unit 5, what distinguishes Christianity is what the Gospel story tells us about Jesus Christ's life and death. But the authority of this distinction rests completely in the resurrection.

In other words, the resurrection authorizes the particular way in which Jesus Christ lived and died as a trustworthy characterization of the God of Israel. The resurrection also authorizes the particular way in which Jesus Christ lived and died as an authentic way for God's people to live and die. In short, the truthfulness of Christian thought and existence rests entirely on whether or not Christ "rose again from the dead" on the third day. This is why Paul asserts to the Corinthians:

> If Christ has not been raised, your faith is futile and you are still in your sins. . . . If for this life only we have hoped in Christ, we are of all people most to be pitied. (1 Cor. 15:17–19, NRSV)

If Jesus Christ has not been raised, the extraordinary way in which Jesus Christ lived and died recedes anonymously into history as yet another fine example—perhaps the finest—in that long line of brave, idealistic, forgettable humanists. But if Jesus Christ *has* been raised, then Jesus Christ has proven that the other side of God's power is strength in the form of weakness. And if the other side of God's power is strength in the form of weakness, then Jesus Christ has also authenticated the church's foolish way of seeking God in the weakness, suffering, and death of others.

> "The growing literature of Christian witness through identification with the poor and the oppressed bears testimony to the reality of a power that prisons and death cannot extinguish."—Williamson, *Mark*, Interpretation, 288.

In this way, the ending is really the beginning for Christianity. Why, then, does Mark tell us so little here at the end?

Overview

Mark's account of the resurrection is stunning. The problem is, we rarely allow Mark to speak on his own terms. The story of the resurrection (like the stories of Jesus' birth and death) is a story more often remembered and retold as an amalgamation of Matthew, Mark, Luke, and John. But in fusing four distinct witnesses, the church loses the richness of four gifted artists, each rendering the same subject from a distinct point of view. Would we not stand aghast if someone cut and pasted pieces of our personal portrait from four great painters onto one canvas? How is it that we are so much more lenient with the Gospel portraits of Jesus Christ? We will encounter far more of the truth if we give each of the Gospel witnesses a deliberate hearing before we bring them to the table together.

When we do this—when we listen to the Gospel storytellers individually—we rediscover the tantalizing eccentricity of Mark. We are so devoted to the other Gospel accounts and to their intriguing "variations" on his theme that we have lost sight of Mark's capacity for arresting narrative invention. Perhaps we have neglected Mark because he never lets us off easy, either as disciples of Jesus Christ or as readers of the Gospel story. This is especially true with the ultimate story of triumph, Mark's account of the resurrection. "Those who seek, in the resurrection, closure for the story of Jesus and a program for the mission of the church should turn to another

Gospel," warns Williamson (286), "The significance of Mark 16:1–8 lies instead in its understanding of the basic life-stance of a Christian: expectancy."

Mark is acutely aware that Jesus' resurrection is the linchpin of this whole story. Yet when Mark comes to the sine qua non of this narrative moment, he carefully crafts it so that we are satisfied but eager, fulfilled but expectant, confident but not overconfident, and fearful but willing. For Mark, more than for the other Gospel writers, *delayed gratification* is the backdrop of the resurrection because delayed gratification is the defining challenge for Christian discipleship.

> "[The resurrection] must have seemed as ridiculous as some of the tall tales that are presented as 'news' in our supermarket tabloids."—Hare, *Mark*, Westminster Bible Companion, 223.

In telling of the resurrection, Mark exercises three overarching narrative strategies: (1) restraint, (2) absence, and (3) dislocation.

A Strategy of Restraint

Unlike the other Gospel writers, Mark exercises enormous reserve in his account of the "eighth day of creation." He renders the whole thriller in just eight verses. He allows just three human persons on his Easter stage, all women. There is only one angel, although mysteriously not identified as such; he is only a young man in a white robe. The women are not permitted to break from an emotional state of alarm, confusion, and fear. The angel simply reassures that Jesus of Nazareth has been raised; then commands them to tell Jesus' disciples that Jesus is preceding them to Galilee, where he will await their viewing, just

> "The fact that it is women who are portrayed as the first witnesses of Jesus' resurrection underlines the historical truth of the story, for no one in that culture would have invented a story that gave such a key role to women."—Donald A. Hagner, in *Life in the Face of Death: The Resurrection Message in the New Testament*, edited by Richard Longnecker (Grand Rapids: Wm. B. Eerdmans Publishing Co., 1998), 109.

as he said. And that's it. That's all there is in Mark's eight-verse Easter.

Let us now examine what is missing from Mark's account (see the table on page 116). Notice in particular how abnormal and nonstandard Mark's account has become for the church.

Matthew	Luke	John
A great earthquake An angel rolling the stone Guards paralyzed by fear An assembly of the Jewish council to bribe the guards to spread the rumor that the disciples stole Jesus' body	Two men in dazzling apparel chastising the women The women returning to tell the disciples, slamming into their skepticism Peter madly rushing to the cemetery Linen cloths lying Cleopas and another walking to Emmaus on Easter afternoon A fish fry	A sole appearance by Mary Magdalene, who returns to Peter and the "one whom Jesus loved" decrying the theft of Jesus' body Peter and the beloved racing on foot to the tomb A rolled-up head napkin Mary weeping Two angels in white sympathizing with Mary A misidentified gardener

Mark lacks all of the above. He completes the scene and brings his Gospel story to a close in eight short verses. Matthew takes twenty verses; Luke needs fifty-three; and John wows us with fifty-six verses of the day of the resurrection and beyond.

A Strategy of Absence

As surprising as the above omissions are, the single most startling omission from Mark's Easter is Jesus. *Nobody directly experiences the risen Jesus!* He neither actively appears nor is he passively sighted by a single person; he is merely alluded to by a youngster in a white suit.

"His absence signals his presence in unimagined realities."—John P. Keenan, *The Gospel of Mark: A Mayahana Reading* (Maryknoll, N.Y.: Orbis Books, 1995), 393.

In Matthew's account, the eleven disciples go to Galilee and not only see Jesus but worship him and listen to his sermon on making disciples of all nations. In Luke's version, Jesus slides in alongside the wayfaring disciples on the road to Emmaus and opens their eyes at supper; then he appears to the whole group and calms their fear of ghosts, enjoys a fish fry, and blesses them just before he is whisked up into heaven. Lastly, in John's story, Jesus surprises tearful Mary in the cemetery at dawn, passes through locked doors to calm the disciples at dusk, and offers his wounds to doubting Thomas; then a week later, Jesus enjoys a clambake with his disciples while quizzing them about their devotion to him. Against these elaborate encounters with the resurrected Jesus, Mark's account seems very lean indeed. We get no closer to Jesus on Easter than a stranger's promise.

A Strategy of Disruption

Believe it or not, Mark ends his entire Gospel story smack in the middle of a sentence, with a little explanatory conjunction dangling in thin air. Whoever said it was grammatically incorrect to end a sentence with a preposition would be flabbergasted by Mark. If sentence-ending prepositions are grammatically incorrect, then Mark commits grammatical treason.

Almost all English translations smooth over this uncomfortably awkward concluding sentence, but in doing so they dishonestly rearrange the Greek text. In fact, it is so unnerving that ancient copy scribes took the liberty to amend Mark's ending in a variety of ways. That's why different endings are denoted in most English translations as "Shorter Ending" and "Longer Ending," and why there are copious explanatory footnotes. But let it be clear, the Greek text of Mark's final sentence (16:8) in the most authoritative manuscripts for the New Testament literally reads: "And [the women] said nothing to anyone; they were fearing, for . . . " There it is, in all its disruptive baldness, to tantalize the church forever. The narrator just walks off the stage while talking! The words we miss are the very words we wish most to hear. But the narrator is gone. The story has ended. Or has it?

Let us restate the situation. The historic, oldest Gospel story of Jesus Christ ends incompletely with a conjunction. Only *The Bible in Basic English* (1949/64) captures the punch of Mark's ending: "And they went out quickly from the place, because fear and great wonder had come on them: and they said nothing to anyone, because they were full of fear that . . . " This ending has been described by the British New Testament

> "Mark's story of Jesus' ministry, passion, resurrection terminates abruptly with fear, flight, and silence."—Hare, *Mark*, Westminster Bible Companion, 222.

scholar D. E. Nineham as no less than "the greatest of all literary mysteries" (Nineham, 439).

An Unfinished Ending

While it is true that Mark's account of the resurrection is told in only eight verses, he does very clearly and concretely witness to the resurrection of Jesus of Nazareth. The witness is placed on the lips of the (angelic) young man and it is indisputable: "He was raised" (v. 6). Williamson (284) identifies this message as "the heart of this unit and the key to the entire Gospel. . . . The message brings dramatic reversal to a tragic narrative that had seemed to end in the abandonment and death of the Son of God." Unlike the musical *Jesus Christ Superstar*, the Gospel of Mark plainly contains the resurrection. Mark is not out to challenge the rising of Jesus Christ from the dead, either as event or as doctrine. Perhaps it helps to liken the resurrection to pregnancy. All it takes is a little. Mark's "little" is sufficient.

Mark's aim in this extraordinary telling is to provoke the church to complete this unfinished ending. As he has painfully highlighted throughout the narrative, the only sensible place for the disciples to be is behind Jesus, willfully following, wherever he precedes and at whatever price he requires. This is why Mark leaves us with this remarkable picture of the church as a community whose Lord has preceded us and is graciously awaiting our obedience. The "great commission" in Mark is simply to follow Jesus to Galilee, the place where he does public ministry. The inspiration to do so is simply his promise that we will see him. It's not much, but Mark has been singing this no-gimmick song of discipleship throughout the story.

Here at the end, Mark gives the proclamation of the Gospel to "a young man, dressed in a white robe, sitting on the right side," presumably an angel (16:5, NRSV). The young man's proclamation contains a threefold command, a correction, and a promise (16:6–7). To the three distressed women, he commands, "Be not alarmed . . . Go . . . Tell." Then the young man corrects, or better, redirects them, "The Jesus of Nazareth you seek—the crucified one—is no longer here; Jesus of Nazareth is now the *raised*, cru-

> "Looking among the dead for one crucified, the women are assured that they are looking in the wrong place."—Williamson, *Mark*, Interpretation, 284.

cified one." Finally, he promises, or more accurately, conveys Jesus' promise, "You will see him when you follow him" (16:7).

The last thing we are told is that the women do indeed go, but we are left wondering about their obedience. Mark states the women's predicament rather strongly, going out of his way to picture them as fleeing in a state of siege: "They went out and fled from the tomb, for trembling and disorientation were seizing them, and they said not one thing to anyone; they were being afraid, you see" (16:8). Is this a picture of apprehensive obedience or of outright defection? The text seems to point to the latter, as Williamson affirms (285), "The last verse . . . falls like a bomb on the carefully nurtured expectation that the women will always faithfully do what needs to be done. . . . The one group of faithful followers finally fails." Mark appears to be leaving the church with this disturbing picture of itself locked in confusion, fleeing the divine command and abandoning the hope of Jesus' promise.

The key to Mark's purpose, however, is his sustained conviction that a disciple of the crucified Messiah will experience him as the *resurrected,* crucified Messiah whenever he or she risks everything, steps out, and follows. This is precisely why Williamson (285) and, increasingly, New Testament scholarship finds

> "No ending proposed by our decisions can contain him, any more than the tomb with its great stone could."—Williamson, *Mark,* Interpretation, 286.

Mark's unfinished ending provocative and purposeful: "Mark's ending is no end; only the reader can bring closure." All that the church can know with confidence is that the raised, crucified one is preceding us into the world, promising to become visible in our following. "To see Jesus the women and the disciples must look ahead" (Williamson, 284). Mark is calling for a church that appreciates the inherently incomplete nature of the Gospel story, a community of disciples that will deny itself, pick up its cross, and risk finishing the story.

True, unlike the other Gospel authors, Mark leaves us in a disturbing predicament on Easter morning. How dare he cast a pall over this glorious day. But Mark's bottom line is that the church gets no peek at glory prior to

📖 Want to Know More?

About resurrection? See Shirley C. Guthrie, *Christian Doctrine,* rev. ed. (Louisville, Ky.: Westminster John Knox Press, 1994), 270–88.

About the ending of the Gospel of Mark? See Eduard Schweizer, *The Good News According to Mark* (Atlanta: John Knox Press, 1970), 363–79.

risking its life. The church gets only a word from Jesus and a half-drawn picture of itself. The word comforts and the picture vexes.

The word is that the crucified one lives and precedes the church, just as he promised. But the picture suggests that we are afraid to complete the story and discover this for ourselves.

Is this the truth about us?

? Questions for Reflection

1. In discussing Mark's account of the resurrection, the unit says, "We get no closer to Jesus on Easter than a stranger's promise." What are ways one gets close to Jesus? Is it more than someone else's word? Why or why not?
2. If the ending of Mark as we have it is correct, and we are left dangling with an unfinished thought, what are some ways you would complete the wording of verse 8?
3. The women fled in fear. Using a concordance, look up other occurrences of fear, fright, and terror in Mark's Gospel. What are the occasions that generate fear? Is fear a right response or a wrong response? Why?
4. In one or two sentences, how would you summarize the basic message of the Gospel of Mark? In the first unit, you were asked to give an understanding of the phrase "good news." Now, at the completion of the study, what changes might you make to that understanding?

Bibliography

Barclay, William. *The Gospel of Mark.* Daily Study Bible. Rev. ed. Philadelphia: Westminster Press, 1975.

Barth, Karl. *The Epistle to the Romans,* 6th ed. Translated by Edwin C. Hoskyns. Oxford: Oxford University Press, 1933.

Book of Confessions. Part I of the Constitution of the Presbyterian Church (U.S.A.). Louisville, Ky.: The Office of the General Assembly, 1996.

Book of Order 1998–1999. Part II of the Constitution of the Presbyterian Church (U.S.A.). Louisville, Ky.: The Office of the General Assembly, 1998.

Calvin, John. *Commentary on a Harmony of the Evangelists, Matthew, Mark, and Luke,* vol. 1, translated by William Pringle. Repr. Grand Rapids: Baker Book House, 1989.

Elliot, Elisabeth. *Shadow of the Almighty: The Life and Testament of Jim Elliot.* San Francisco: Harper & Row, 1956.

Hare, Douglass R. A. *Mark.* Westminster Bible Companion. Louisville, Ky.: Westminster John Knox Press, 1966.

Minear, Paul S. *Mark.* The Layman's Bible Commentary. Atlanta: John Knox Press, 1960.

Moltmann, Jürgen. *The Crucified God: The Cross of Christ as the Foundation and Criticism of Christian Theology.* Translated by R. A. Wilson and John Bowden. New York: Harper & Row, 1973.

Nickle, Keith F. *The Synoptic Gospels: An Introduction.* Atlanta: John Knox Press, 1980.

Nietzsche, Friedrich. *The Anti-Christ,* aphorism 39 (1895). In *Twilight of the Idols; and the Anti-Christ.* Translated by R.J. Hollingdale. Baltimore: Penguin Books, 1968.

Nineham, D. E. *Saint Mark.* Westminster Pelican Commentaries. Philadelphia: Westminster Press, 1978.

Rist, Martin. "Apocalypticism," *The Interpreter's Dictionary of the Bible,* Volume A–D. Nashville: Abingdon Press, 1962.

The Bible in Basic English. Cambridge: Cambridge University Press, 1949/ 1964.

Williamson, Lamar, Jr. *Mark.* Interpretation. Atlanta: John Knox Press, 1983.

Interpretation Bible Studies
Leader's Guide

Interpretation Bible Studies (IBS), for adults and older youth, are flexible, attractive, easy-to-use, and filled with solid information about the Bible. IBS helps Christians discover the guidance and power of the scriptures for living today. Perhaps you are leading a church school class, a mid-week Bible study group, or a youth group meeting, or simply using this in your own personal study. Whatever the setting may be, we hope you find this *Leader's Guide* helpful. Since every context and group is different, this *Leader's Guide* does not presume to tell you how to structure Bible study for your situation. Instead, the *Leader's Guide* seeks to offer choices—a number of helpful suggestions for leading a successful Bible study using IBS.

> "The church that no longer hears the essential message of the Scriptures soon ceases to understand what it is for and is open to be captured by the dominant religious philosophy of the moment." —James D. Smart, *The Strange Silence of the Bible in the Church: A Study in Hermeneutics* (Philadelphia: Westminster Press, 1970), 10.

How Should I Teach IBS?

1. Explore the Format

There is a wealth of information in IBS, perhaps more than you can use in one session. In this case, more is better. IBS has been designed to give you a well-stocked buffet of content and teachable insights. Pick and choose what suits your group's needs. Perhaps you will want to split units into two or more sessions, or combine units into a single session. Perhaps you will decide to use only a portion of a unit and then move on to the next unit. *There is not a structured theme or teaching focus to each unit that must be followed for IBS to be used.* Rather, IBS offers the flexibility to adjust to whatever suits your context.

> "The more we bring to the Bible, the more we get from the Bible." —William Barclay, *A Beginner's Guide to the New Testament* (Louisville, Ky.: Westminster John Knox Press, 1995), vii.

A recent survey of both professional and volunteer church educators revealed that their number one concern was that Bible study materials be teacher-friendly. IBS is, indeed teacher-friendly in two important ways. First, since IBS provides abundant content and a flexible design, teachers can shape the lessons creatively, responding to the needs of the group and employing a wide variety of teaching methods. Second, those who wish more specific suggestions for planning the sessions can find them at the Geneva Press web site on the Internet (**www.ppcpub.org**). Click the "IBS Teacher Helps" button to access teaching suggestions for each IBS unit as well as helpful quotations, selections from Bible dictionaries and encyclopedias, and other teaching helps.

IBS is also not only teacher-friendly, it is also discussion-friendly. Given the opportunity, most adults and young people relish the chance to talk about the kind of issues raised in IBS. The secret, then, is to determine what works with your group, what will get them to talk. Several good methods for stimulating discussion are presented in this *Leader's Guide,* and once you learn your group, you can apply one of these methods and get the group discussing the Bible and its relevance in their lives.

The format of every IBS unit consists of several features:

a. Body of the Unit. This is the main content, consisting of interesting and informative commentary on the passage and scholarly insight into the biblical text and its significance for Christians today.

b. Sidebars. These are boxes that appear scattered throughout the body of the unit, with maps, photos, quotations, and intriguing ideas. Some sidebars can be identified quickly by a symbol, or icon, that helps the reader know what type of information can be found in that sidebar. There are icons for illustrations, key terms, pertinent quotes, and more.

c. Want to Know More? Each unit includes a "Want to Know More?" section that guides learners who wish to dig deeper and consult other resources. If your church library does not have the resources mentioned, you can look up the information in other standard Bible dictionaries, encyclopedias, and handbooks, or you can find much of this information at the Geneva Press Web site (see page 92).

d. Questions for Reflection. The unit ends with questions to help the learners think more deeply about the biblical passage and its pertinence for today. These questions are provided as examples only, and teachers are encouraged both to develop their own list of questions and to gather questions from the group. These discussion questions do not usually have specific "correct" answers. Again, the flexibility of IBS allows you to use these questions at the end of the group time, at the beginning, interspersed throughout, or not at all.

> "The trick is to make the Bible our book." —
> Duncan S. Ferguson, *Bible Basics: Mastering the Content of the Bible* (Louisville, Ky.: Westminster John Knox Press, 1995), 3.

2. Select a Teaching Method

Here are ten suggestions. The format of IBS allows you to choose what direction you will take as you plan to teach. Only you will know how your lesson should best be designed for your group. Some adult groups prefer the lecture method, while others prefer a high level of free-ranging discussion. Many youth groups like interaction, activity, the use of music, and the chance to talk about their own experiences and feelings. Here is a list of a few possible approaches. Let your own creativity add to the list!

a. Let's Talk about What We've Learned. In this approach, all group members are requested to read the scripture passage and the IBS unit before the group meets. Ask the group members to make notes about the main issues, concerns, and questions they see in the passage. When the group meets, these notes are collected, shared, and discussed. This method depends, of course, on the group's willingness to do some "homework."

b. What Do We Want and Need to Know? This approach begins by having the whole group read the scripture passage together. Then, drawing from your study of the IBS, you, as the teacher, write on a board or flip chart two lists:

(1) Things we should know to better understand this passage (content information related to the passage, for example, historical insights about political contexts, geographical landmarks, economic nuances, etc.) and

(2) Four or five "important issues we should talk about regarding this passage" (with implications for today—how the issues in the biblical context continue into today, for example, issues of idolatry or fear). Allow the group to add to either list, if they wish, and use the lists to lead into a time of learning, reflection, and discussion. This approach is suitable for those settings where there is little or no advanced preparation by the students.

> "Although small groups can meet for many purposes and draw upon many different resources, the one resource which has shaped the life of the Church more than any other throughout its long history has been the Bible." —Roberta Hestenes, *Using the Bible in Groups* (Philadelphia: Westminster Press, 1983), 14.

c. Hunting and Gathering. Start the unit by having the group read the scripture passage together. Then divide the group into smaller clusters (perhaps having as few as one person), each with a different assignment. Some clusters can discuss one or more of the "Questions for Reflection." Others can look up key terms or people in a Bible dictionary or track down other biblical references found in the body of the unit. After the small clusters have had time to complete their tasks, gather the entire group again and lead them through the study material, allowing each cluster to contribute what it learned.

d. From Question Mark to Exclamation Point. This approach begins with contemporary questions and then moves to the biblical content as a response to those questions. One way to do this is for you to ask the group, at the beginning of the class, a rephrased version of one or more of the "Questions for Reflection" at the end of the study unit. For example, one of the questions at the end of the unit on Exodus 3:1–4:17 in the IBS *Exodus* volume reads,

> Moses raised four protests, or objections, to God's call. Contemporary people also raise objections to God's call. In what ways are these similar to Moses' protests? In what ways are they different?

This question assumes familiarity with the biblical passage about Moses, so the question would not work well before the group has explored the passage. However, try rephrasing this question as an opening exercise; for example:

Here is a thought experiment: Let's assume that God, who called people in the Bible to do daring and risky things, still calls people today to tasks of faith and courage. In the Bible, God called Moses from a burning bush and called Isaiah in a moment of ecstatic worship in the Temple. How do you think God's call is experienced by people today? Where do you see evidence of people saying "yes" to God's call? When people say "no" or raise an objection to God's call, what reasons do they give (to themselves, to God)?

Posing this or a similar question at the beginning will generate discussion and raise important issues, and then it can lead the group into an exploration of the biblical passage as a resource for thinking even more deeply about these questions.

e. Let's Go to the Library. From your church library, your pastor's library, or other sources, gather several good commentaries on the book of the Bible you are studying. Among the trustworthy commentaries are those in the Interpretation series (John Knox Press) and the Westminster Bible Companion series (Westminster John Knox Press). Divide your group into smaller clusters and give one commentary to each cluster (one or more of the clusters can be given the IBS volume instead of a full-length commentary). Ask each cluster to read the biblical passage you are studying and then to read the section of the commentary that covers that passage (if your group is large, you may want to make photocopies of the commentary material with proper permission, of course). The task of each cluster is to name the two or three most important insights they discover about the biblical passage by reading and talking together about the commentary material. When you reassemble the larger group to share these insights, your group will gain not only a variety of insights about the passage but also a sense that differing views of the same text are par for the course in biblical interpretation.

f. Working Creatively Together. Begin with a creative group task, tied to the main thrust of the study. For example, if the study is on the Ten Commandments, a parable, or a psalm, have the group rewrite the Ten Commandments, the parable, or the psalm in contemporary language. If the passage is an epistle, have the group write a letter to their own congregation. Or if the study is a narrative, have the group role-play the characters in the story or write a page describing the story from the point of view of one of the characters. After completion of the task, read and discuss the biblical passage,

127

asking for interpretations and applications from the group and tying in IBS material as it fits the flow of the discussion.

g. Singing Our Faith. Begin the session by singing (or reading) together a hymn that alludes to the biblical passage being studied (or to the theological themes in the passage). Most hymnals have an index of scriptural allusions. For example, if you are studying the unit from the IBS volume on Psalm 121, you can sing "I to the Hills Will Lift My Eyes," "Sing Praise to God, Who Reigns Above," or another hymn based on Psalm 121. Let the group reflect on the thoughts and feelings evoked by the hymn, then move to the biblical passage, allowing the biblical text and the IBS material to underscore, clarify, refine, and deepen the discussion stimulated by the hymn. If you are ambitious, you may ask the group to write a new hymn at the end of the study! (Many hymnals have indexes in the back or companion volumes that help the user match hymns to scripture passages or topics.)

h. Fill in the Blanks. In order to help the learners focus on the content of the biblical passage, at the beginning of the session ask each member of the group to read the biblical passage and fill out a brief questionnaire about the details of the passage (provide a copy for each learner or write the questions on the board). For example, if you are studying the unit in the IBS *Matthew* volume on Matthew 22:1–14, the questionnaire could include questions such as the following:

—In this story, Jesus compares the kingdom of heaven to what?
—List the various responses of those who were invited to the king's banquet but who did not come.
—When his invitation was rejected, how did the king feel? What did the king do?
—In the second part of the story, when the king saw a man at the banquet without a wedding garment, what did the king say? What did the man say? What did the king do?
—What is the saying found at the end of this story?

Gather the group's responses to the questions, perhaps encouraging discussion. Then lead the group through the IBS material helping the learners to understand the meanings of these details and the significance of the passage for today. Feeling creative? Instead of a fill-in-the-blanks questionnaire, create a crossword puzzle from names and words in the biblical passage.

i. Get the Picture. In this approach, stimulate group discussion by incorporating a painting, photograph, or other visual object into the lesson. You can begin by having the group examine and comment on this visual or you can introduce the visual later in the lesson—it depends on the object used. If, for example, you are studying the unit Exodus 3:1–4:17 in the IBS *Exodus* volume, you may want to view Paul Koli's very colorful painting *The Burning Bush*. Two sources for this painting are *The Bible Through Asian Eyes*, edited by Masao Takenaka and Ron O'Grady (National City, Calif.: Pace Publishing Co., 1991), and *Imaging the Word: An Arts and Lectionary Resource*, vol. 3, edited by Susan A. Blain (Cleveland: United Church Press, 1996).

j. Now Hear This. Especially if your class is large, you may want to use the lecture method. As the teacher, you prepare a presentation on the biblical passage, using as many resources as you have available plus your own experience, but following the content of the IBS unit as a guide. You can make the lecture even more lively by asking the learners at various points along the way to refer to the visuals and quotes found in the "sidebars." A place can be made for questions (like the ones at the end of the unit)—either at the close of the lecture or at strategic points along the way.

> "It is . . . important to call a Bible study group back to what the text being discussed actually says, especially when an individual has gotten off on some tangent." —Richard Robert Osmer, *Teaching for Faith: A Guide for Teachers of Adult Classes* (Louisville, Ky.: Westminster John Knox Press, 1992), 71.

3. Keep These Teaching Tips in Mind

There are no surefire guarantees for a teaching success. However, the following suggestions can increase the chances for a successful study:

a. Always Know Where the Group Is Headed. Take ample time beforehand to prepare the material. Know the main points of the study, and know the destination. Be flexible, and encourage discussion, but don't lose sight of where you are headed.

b. Ask Good Questions; Don't Be Afraid of Silence. Ideally, a discussion blossoms spontaneously from the reading of the scripture. But more often than not, a discussion must be drawn from the group members by a series of well-chosen questions. After asking each question, give the group members time to answer. Let them think, and don't be threatened by a season of silence. Don't feel that every question must have an answer, and that as leader, you must supply every answer. Facilitate discussion by getting the group members to cooperate with each other. Sometimes, the original question can be restated. Sometimes it is helpful to ask a follow-up question like "What makes this a hard question to answer?"

Ask questions that encourage explanatory answers. Try to avoid questions that can be answered simply "Yes" or "No." Rather than asking, "Do you think Moses was frightened by the burning bush?" ask, "What do you think Moses was feeling and experiencing as he stood before the burning bush?" If group members answer with just one word, ask a follow-up question like "Why do you think this is so?" Ask questions about their feelings and opinions, mixed within questions about facts or details. Repeat their responses or restate their response to reinforce their contributions to the group.

> "Studies of learning reveal that while people remember approximately 10% of what they hear, they remember up to 90% of what they say. Therefore, to increase the amount of learning that occurs, increase the amount of talking about the Bible which each member does."—Roberta Hestenes, *Using the Bible in Groups* (Philadelphia: Westminster Press, 1983), 17.

Most studies can generate discussion by asking open-ended questions. Depending on the group, several types of questions can work. Some groups will respond well to content questions that can be answered from reading the IBS comments or the biblical passage. Others will respond well to questions about feelings or thoughts. Still others will respond to questions that challenge them to new thoughts or that may not have exact answers. Be sensitive to the group's dynamic in choosing questions.

Some suggested questions are: What is the point of the passage? Who are the main characters? Where is the tension in the story? Why does it say (this)_____, and not (that) _____? What raises questions for you? What terms need defining? What are the new ideas? What doesn't make sense? What bothers or troubles you about this passage? What keeps you from living the truth of this passage?

c. Don't Settle for the Ordinary. There is nothing like a surprise. Think of special or unique ways to present the ideas of the study. Upset the applecart of the ordinary. Even though the passage may be familiar, look for ways to introduce suspense. Remember that a little mystery can capture the imagination. Change your routine.

Along with the element of surprise, humor can open up a discussion. Don't be afraid to laugh. A well-chosen joke or cartoon may present the central theme in a way that a lecture would have stymied.

Sometimes a passage is too familiar. No one speaks up because everyone feels that all that could be said has been said. Choose an unfamiliar translation from which to read, or if the passage is from a Gospel, compare the story across two or more Gospels and note differences. It is amazing what insights can be drawn from seeing something strange in what was thought to be familiar.

d. Feel Free to Supplement the IBS Resources with Other Material. Consult other commentaries or resources. Tie in current events with the lesson. Scour newspapers or magazines for stories that touch on the issues of the study. Sometimes the lyrics of a song, or a section of prose from a well-written novel will be just the right seasoning for the study.

e. And Don't Forget to Check the Web. Check out our site on the World Wide Web (www.ppcpub.org). Click the "IBS Teacher Helps" button to access teaching suggestions. Several possibilities for applying the teaching methods suggested above for individual IBS units will be available. Feel free to download this material.

> "The Bible is literature, but it is much more than literature. It is the holy book of Jews and Christians, who find there a manifestation of God's presence." —Kathleen Norris, *The Psalms* (New York: Riverhead Books, 1997), xxii.

f. Stay Close to the Biblical Text. Don't forget that the goal is to learn the Bible. Return to the text again and again. Avoid making the mistake of reading the passage only at the beginning of the study, and then wandering away to comments on top of comments from that point on. Trust in the power and presence of the Holy Spirit to use the truths of the passage to work within the lives of the study participants.

What If I Am Using IBS in Personal Bible Study?

If you are using IBS in your personal Bible study, you can experiment and explore a variety of ways. You may choose to read straight through the study without giving any attention to the sidebars or other features. Or you may find yourself interested in a question or unfamiliar with a key term, and you can allow the sidebars, "Want to Know More?" and "Questions for Reflection" to lead you into deeper learning on these issues. Perhaps you will want to have a few commentaries or a Bible dictionary available to pursue what interests you. As was suggested in one of the teaching methods above, you may want to begin with the questions at the end, and then read the Bible passage followed by the IBS material. Trust the IBS resources to provide good and helpful information, and then follow your interests!

Want to Know More?

About leading Bible study groups? See Roberta Hestenes, *Using the Bible in Groups* (Philadelphia: Westminster Press, 1983).

About basic Bible content? See Duncan S. Ferguson, *Bible Basics: Mastering the Content of the Bible* (Louisville, Ky.: Westminster John Knox Press, 1995); William M. Ramsay, *The Westminster Guide to the Books of the Bible* (Louisville, Ky.: Westminster John Knox Press, 1994).

About the development of the Bible? See John Barton, *How the Bible Came to Be* (Louisville, Ky.: Westminster John Knox Press, 1997).

About the meaning of difficult terms? See Donald K. McKim, *Westminster Dictionary of Theological Terms* (Louisville, Ky.: Westminster John Knox Press, 1996); Paul J. Achtemeier, *Harper's Bible Dictionary* (San Francisco: Harper & Row, 1985).

For more information about IBS,
click the "IBS Teacher Helps" button at
www.ppcpub.org